BOMBER PILOT

VANWELL
VOICES
of WAR

HARLO L. JONES, DFC, CD

BOMBER PILOT

A CANADIAN YOUTH'S WAR

Vanwell Publishing Limited

St. Catharines, Ontario

Vanwell Publishing acknowledges the financial support of the Government of Canada through the Book Publishing Industry Development Program for our publishing activities.

Design: Linda Moroz-Irvine
Cover: Engineer Wally Wilkins in Halifax VII EQ-R. Below: a Lancaster bomber.

Vanwell Publishing Limited
1 Northrup Crescent
P.O. Box 2131
St. Catharines, Ontario L2R 7S2

Printed in Canada

Canadian Cataloguing in Publication Data

Jones, Harlo L. (Harlo Lloyd), 1923-
        Bomber pilot : a Canadian youth's war

(Vanwell voices of war)
ISBN 1-55125-084-5
ISSN 1498-8844

  1. Jones, Harlo L. (Harlo Lloyd), 1923- . 2. World
War, 1939–Personal narratives, Canadian. 3. World War, 1939-1945–
Aerial operations, Canadian. 4. Bomber pilots–Canada–
Biography. I. Title. II. Series.

D811.J67 2001   940.54'4971'2   C2001-902110-0

ACKNOWLEDGEMENTS

Details of the effects of bombing raids herein described are taken from *The RCAF Overseas: The Fifth Year* and *The RCAF Overseas: The Sixth Year*, both written by the Air Historian's Branch of the Department of National Defence and published by Oxford University Press, Amen House, Toronto, in 1945 and 1949.

I am indebted, for many of the details dealing with electronic measures and countermeasures and their effects on Bomber Command tactics, to R.V. Jones of wartime British Scientific Intelligence, who describes them so well in his book *Most Secret War*, published in Coronet Edition by Hodder and Stoughton Ltd., Mill Road, Dunton Green, Sevenoaks, Kent, in 1979. This is surely one of the most fascinating books ever written about the Second World War. Wartime aircrew have discovered in it the "Why?" of many things we were told to do or not to do.

This book is for my two sons, Maldwyn and Rhys, and my daughter Kathryn, all of whom I love beyond measure and who, if the war had gone differently for me, would never have existed. Their achievements are my greatest pride, and are largely due to the devoted mothering through the years given them joyfully by my dear wife, Ethel.

CHAPTER 1

Beginnings

There was never any doubt in my mind. When I turned eighteen I would join the air force and become a pilot. I wanted nothing more than to follow in the footsteps of my second brother who had joined the Royal Air Force (RAF) early in 1939, and who had become a fighter pilot with 242 Squadron, the RAF's first all-Canadian fighter squadron in the Second World War. Sadly, he was reported missing in action on 28 May 1940 during the British evacuation through Dunkirk. Several months later we learned via the American Red Cross that he had been killed and was buried in a Belgian communal cemetery at Oostduinkerke.

My eighteenth birthday fell on 29 December 1941 so on the morning of 10 January 1942 I presented myself to the Royal Canadian Air Force Recruiting Unit in Saskatoon expecting to be enrolled forthwith. I was immediately faced with a problem. The recruiting office insisted that I have two letters of recommendation testifying to my good character. As our home was in Dinsmore, some 90 miles from Saskatoon and I was attending the University of Saskatchewan, I was at a loss for a time until it occurred to me to ask for the required letters from my father's business acquaintances. I thought of two whose businesses were located within three blocks of the recruiting unit and in a couple of hours I returned with the necessary letters, believing all was now only a formality. How wrong I was.

The next stage in the process was a medical examination and the scales were as far as I got. I was rejected for being underweight. This probably resulted from a rapid increase in growth I experienced between the ages of sixteen and eighteen, during which time I grew about six inches in height to 5ft 10in. Unfortunately, my body didn't fill out at the same pace so I tipped the beam at only one hundred and ten pounds. I was shocked beyond measure. The thought of rejection had never occurred to me.

So, what to do next? I returned to my university classes obsessed with schemes to gain weight. I ate all of the rich and fattening foods I could find at all hours of the day and well into the night. I considered manufacturing for myself, in some fashion, a pair of lead-lined shorts with which to fool the medical officer but I was defeated by the impracticality of combining enough weight with the flexibility and invisibility required at certain stages of the examination. I gave up on that idea. I wondered what weight of food one could eat or what heavy but harmless material one could ingest just prior to another medical so as to add a few pounds.

Unfortunately, my food bingeing was to no avail. The scales stubbornly refused to register any gain. So, on 10 February, I once more presented myself to the recruiting unit with some trepidation. This time, I encountered a much more sympathetic medic who opined that I undoubtedly would gain weight while in the Service and with a muttered, "You skinny bastards will outlive the rest of us anyway," put my weight down as 118 pounds and gave me an aircrew medical category. I was in, or at least I was assured of being accepted. As I expressed the wish to finish the university year, I was allowed to return on 10 April to be enrolled and put on leave without pay until the end of the university year. I left the recruiting unit walking on air but facing the unpleasant necessity of telling my parents what I had done. I suspected that having lost one son, and with my older brother already in the RCAF, my mother and father would not take kindly to my action, particularly as I was in a university programme that protected me from being called up. In the event it was accepted by them, almost fatalistically.

During my two years at university I had had some exposure to the military. During first year, all male students were obliged to take some military training in what was termed the Auxiliary Battalion of the Canadian Officers Training Corps (COTC). In second year one was eligible to join the COTC as a cadet, which I did. We were given drill as well as lectures which counted toward a course credit and at the end of the year we wrote an examination which, if we passed, qualified us as Second Lieutenant, Infantry Rifle. The desperate shortage of military equipment for the active army was evidenced by our training equipment—American surplus Springfield rifles with 14-inch "breadknife" bayonets, a World War I Lewis machine gun and a .5 inch Boyes anti-tank rifle which would have been as effective against German tanks of the day as a pea shooter.

Training took place under the direction of a rather elderly Major in the active army who had a pronounced English accent and who often boarded the same streetcar as I. He would return my greeting me with a "Good Morning" which, as the year progressed became "Good morning, Jones." A short time after the qualifying examination, which was held in advance of the regular university exams, we encountered one another again and a conversation ensued which I recall went something like this:

> I: "Good morning, sir." He: " Good morning Jones. What did you think of the qualifying examination?" I: "Not too bad, Sir." He: "I can tell you, Jones. You did all right, you did all right." I: "Thank you, Sir." He: "Are you going active?" I: "Yes, sir." He: "Good for you. What regiment?" I: "I've joined the air force."

A look of shocked incredulity swept over his face. He turned away and never spoke to me again on that or any other day. On 10 April I reported to the recruiting unit, was attested, accepted the King's shilling (a Canadian dollar) and was duly enrolled in the RCAF as a "P or O," that is "Pilot or Observer," with the exalted rank of Aircraftman Second Class (AC2), the lowest rung on the RCAF ladder of rank. I was put on leave without pay and told to report to the recruiting unit for transportation to Manning Depot on May 27, with only the necessary minimum of civilian clothing. I was also asked to sign a document stating that while on leave without pay, I would conduct myself always in a manner that would bring credit to the RCAF, and that the RCAF would not be financially responsible for any medical or other care I might require or for transportation expense to the recruiting unit other than by the most direct route from my home.

When May 27 rolled around I reported as instructed and with three other recruits was equipped with a coach-class train ticket and a meal ticket for the evening meal on the train. We were escorted to the Canadian National Railroad station in Saskatoon, about two and one-half blocks from the recruiting unit. We boarded the CN transcontinental train with instructions to get off at Brandon North Station where we would be met and transported to 2 Manning Depot.

We arranged ourselves on two facing seats and proceeded to get acquainted. Two of my three companions were former National Hockey League players, Johnny Chad and Archie Wilder, of the Chicago Black Hawks and Detroit Red Wings. The third was a Saskatchewan farm boy whose name has escaped me. Chad and Wilder were an immediate source of instruction to us on the intricacies of train travel. For example, when we went into the diner, they told us that by adding cash to the value of our meal tickets we could have anything on the menu instead of the cheaper meal which, our tickets covered. We dined on steaks.

We arrived at Brandon North Station early in the morning of 28 May, two years to the day after my brother had been killed. We were transported by truck to the Manning Depot along with several others who had arrived on the same train from other locations. We were immediately escorted to the mess for breakfast and our arrival in civilian dress was greeted by a host of uniformed trainees chorusing, "You'll be sor-ree!"

For the first week or so we were "confined to barracks" to be sure we were not incubating any communicable diseases. We were paraded to various areas of what had been the Brandon Exhibition's horse and cattle barns and show ring, all under one roof. We were equipped with uniforms and other kit, shorn by the barbers and ran the barrage of medical needles for tests, inoculations and vaccinations. We had been assigned to bunks on the upper floor of the two-floor horse and cattle barn, our "room" containing four hundred double-tiered bunks.

I claimed an upper bunk, thus elevating myself out of the jungle of angle-iron bunk supports and big blue kit bags, two hanging from the upper rail at the foot of each double-stacked bunk. Along the long east wall of the room plumbing had been installed so there were long stretches of wash basins broken at intervals by partitioned shower rooms, each containing about a dozen showers in a common area—no cubicles. This lack of privacy bothered some, but those of us who had grown up skinny-dipping in dams and dugouts felt no embarrassment.

We were wakened each morning by a bugler playing Reveille, prompting a rush for the wash basins. It was this morning ritual that drew our attention to Archie Wilder as the product of a different mold. While the rest of us performed our morning ablutions we would notice him sitting on his already made-up bunk, polishing his buttons or boots, having showered and shaved before the bugle call. We decided that in the words of a popular song he must be "...that other pup, the guy who wakes the bugler up."

The morning ritual, and the daily polishing of brass buttons and black boots, included stripping our bunks to the mattress and folding blankets and sheets to exactly the same width as the mattress and then placing them at the head of the bunk, folded so the red stripe in the centre of each sheet lined up precisely with the black central stripes woven into the grey blankets. With these chores attended to, we were off to breakfast and then to the parade ground where we spent most of our days in what seemed endless hours of drill.

But early in our time at Brandon, we were given a day off. This was because we were administered an inoculation about which we had been warned by some of those who had preceded us. This was the dreaded TABT. Our flight was paraded to the inoculation area and each of us received what seemed like an enormous shot in the left arm below the shoulder which, we were told, would protect us from two types of typhoid fever and tetanus or "lockjaw". After the inoculation we were designated as "Attend C" for twenty-four hours, a medical term meaning no duties. We were told to return to our quarters and remain quiet to avoid any serious after-effects.

Most obeyed amid groans and moans as the shots took effect and our upper arms began to ache. However, led by Johnny Chad, several of us proceeded to the canteen where we spent most of the day playing table tennis. After the canteen bar opened, we imbibed two or three beers. We suffered no ill effects and very little soreness in our arms. It was obvious when we returned to our quarters we were in much better condition than those who had spent the afternoon on their bunks. One of our group who had remained quiet was removed to sick quarters in the middle of the night, delirious and with a raging fever.

Trainees were assigned to "flights" of about thirty men, and each flight was assigned to a particular noncommissioned officer (NCO) disciplinarian or "discip." Our flight was fortunate in having as our mentor a Corporal Miles, a big man with a friendly manner and a good sense of humour. He had the rare ability to be able to engender enthusiasm and spirit into what otherwise would have been a tremendously boring experience. As a result, our flight became very good at drill. One day he demonstrated both his mastery of drill and our ability to respond by taking us to the tennis courts at one end of the parade square and putting us through every flight manoeuvre in the drill manual. Not one man stepped outside the tapes of half a tennis court.

When it came time for us to learn rifle drill, again with Springfield rifles and 14-inch bayonets, my previous COTC training rescued me from much of the onerous drill. I was assigned by the Corporal to assist him by checking the performance of the others and correcting their errors as he gave the commands. Unfortunately for me, when the others became adept my soft job disappeared.

One thing Corporal Miles disliked was route marches. That is, a hike of anything up to two or three miles. We embarked on one on a June day that was sunny and hot. We were marched to a point where we were out of sight of the Manning Depot and were halted in front of a variety store which dealt in soft drinks, ice cream and magazines. We were broken off with the warning that any one of us who stuck his nose out of the shop for the next hour would be in serious trouble with

Miles. After a suitable interval we were fallen in and marched back to the parade ground—in remarkably good shape for a flight that was supposed to have just completed a three-mile march on a blisteringly hot day!

Then came an inspection by the Air Officer Commanding (AOC) Training Command. There was a great polishing of buttons and boots and pressing of the hated khaki drill summer uniforms which never seemed to hold a crease in the trousers for more than a few minutes. Someone gave out the information that soap rubbed inside the creases before ironing would stiffen them so the crease would stay. I never tried it but one who did, using red Lifebuoy soap, achieved a very spectacular result!

Almost all the personnel of the Manning Depot were on parade, formed up with squadrons in line, the front flight of each squadron equipped with rifles and bayonets to honour the AOC with the "Present Arms." All was in readiness. The AOC's staff car drove up to the gate of the parade ground. At that moment a jackrabbit appeared at one end of the line of squadrons and hippety-hopped at a leisurely pace along the length of the front ranks which were silently and rigidly at attention. As it neared the centre squadron of the seven or eight on parade, one airman in the front rank brought his rifle with fixed bayonet to his shoulder, aimed at the rabbit and shouted, "Bang!" at the top of his voice. The entire parade, and the AOC as well, roared with laughter. The rabbit accelerated to maximum boost and revs, and streaked the rest of the way across the parade ground and out of sight.

The Station Warrant Officer (SWO) marched rapidly toward the airman to take his name and number, but this only added to our amusement as the SWO was a short man whose upper body was longer than his legs giving him a strange gait. We used to joke (not in his hearing) that he was going to sue the city of Brandon for building its sidewalks too close to his ass!

On Sundays we were free to wander the streets of Brandon but there was little to do with nearly all of the shops and places of amusement closed for the Sabbath. However in one establishment which was open we found a coin-operated machine which would stamp out lettering around two-inch soft metal discs. Several of us stamped out our regimental numbers and names on these. I made two, one of which I kept and the other I later gave to the girl who, after the war, became my wife. Fifty years later we still have them.

On a Sunday, too, another AC2 and I decided that if we were going to be aircrew we should get some flying experience. We hitch-hiked to 12 Service Flying Training School (12 SFTS) north of Brandon, convinced the Service Police at the gate that we were harmless, and made our way to the hangars and one of the flight rooms. There we encountered a sympathetic instructor who agreed to take us on an instructional flight. He scrounged a couple of parachutes for us and led us out to a Cessna Crane where a student pilot was waiting. We boarded the aircraft in great excitement and were strapped into the back canvas seat, sitting on our parachute packs.

We grinned at one another in happy anticipation as the aircraft was taxied to the end of the runway and the run-up was done. The aircraft quivered violently as each engine was opened up to full throttle and the magnetos tested. At last the aircraft turned onto the runway, lined up and stopped. We were mystified when the student pilot got out a large roll of canvas, then we exchanged somewhat worried looks as he began to put it on fasteners so it completely blocked his view through the windscreen and to both sides. What had we got ourselves into? We hadn't bargained on riding with a student pilot doing a "blind" take-off.

Finally all was prepared and the student opened the throttles, his gaze fixed on the instrument panel before him. The aircraft picked up speed and the tail lifted. From my seat on the right side I could see the starboard wheel edging closer to the side of the runway and braced myself for what I thought could turn out to be a crash. With my white-knuckled hands gripping the edge of the seat I watched the wheel and then, just as it should have hit the gravel strip along the edge of the runway, I realized it was off the ground. We were airborne.

The rest of the flight was a delight. As the instructor put the student through various drills "under the hood," my companion and I thrilled at the unique view of the countryside as it tilted and revolved around us when the aircraft banked and turned this way and that. Too soon the plane touched down on the runway again and our flight was over. Starry-eyed, we made our way back to the Manning Depot where we were the envy of our comrades when we told them of our adventure.

My only previous flying experience had been when I was about ten years old. Our family was visiting on the farm of an uncle in Nebraska when a barnstormer landed in one of my uncle's fields. A barnstormer in those days was usually an almost penniless flyer who toured the country selling airplane rides to make a living and to support his ambition to fly. In return for the use of the field he offered a free ride to my uncle and two of his family. My uncle, a cousin and I were jammed into the front cockpit of a Swallow biplane and were flown around the town of Wymore. My memories of the flight still are vivid, particularly that of the railroad yards and roundhouse which looked like toys spread out beneath us.

We landed, the barnstormer took on two adult male passengers and headed off again. As the plane rose above the trees at the end of the field its engine quit and it disappeared from our view. Everyone rushed across the corn stubble to the next field and there saw the airplane lying on its back, its rudder crushed, propeller broken, and the top wing and interplane struts buckled. The pilot had made a safe landing but a ditch had caught the wheels after touchdown and flipped the aircraft over. It was a write-off. However, neither the pilot nor his two passengers were hurt. Since that day, I have wondered often what became of the pilot. In the midst of the "dirty thirties" that airplane was probably the only thing in the world he owned. The incident did nothing to dim my interest in planes and flying and now, in the Manning Depot and after the flight at the SFTS, I felt I was on the verge of realizing that dream.

One event at Manning Depot stands out. This was a dance held in what had been the show ring of the exhibition barns and which now, floored over, served as a parade ground, movie theatre and dance floor. What made the event outstanding was the orchestra, led by none other than the famous trumpeter Louis Armstrong. Those of us who for years had played his records on the juke boxes were spellbound and spent much of the dance standing close to the bandstand admiring his artistry and that of his group — "Satchmo" always with his gleaming trumpet held in a white handkerchief.

And there were girls to dance with. How they got there, I don't know. Whether they were brought in from the town by the Air Force or whether they came on their own initiative I don't recall but I spent a good part of the evening dancing with an attractive brunette of my own age who was an excellent partner. We enjoyed dancing with one another.

When the dance was over those of us who had found partners were allowed an hour to escort them home before we had to be back in the barracks. We strolled to her home through the warm summer night and onto her front porch. With a chaste kiss, our acquaintanceship ended.

The evening had one more adventure for me. On re-entering the Manning Depot I was stopped by the SPs for wearing non-issue shoes. At that time the air force issued to us "other ranks" only heavy black boots which definitely were not dancing slippers. I had kept with me a pair of black oxfords I had worn with my civilian clothes when I arrived at the depot and had worn them to the dance. A sharp-eyed SP noticed them and threatened to put me on charge but, after a stern lecture on military dress, he told me to get back to the quarters. I swear he had a twinkle in his eye when he let me go.

That parade square-cum-theatre-cum-dance hall stands out in my memory for another reason. One night I had retired to my bunk early and soon was sound asleep. Suddenly I wakened and was thoroughly confused because I was standing on my feet in a location I didn't recognize, surrounded by sound and flickering light. It must have been several minutes before my befuddled brain locked on to my location. I was standing in the tiered seats behind the movie screen at the opposite end of the show ring from our quarters. Fortunately, the movie audience was seated on chairs on the main floor and I was able to make my way quietly along the upper rows of seats and regain my quarters apparently without my pyjama-clad figure being noticed by anyone. It was the only time in my life I have sleep-walked.

After fifty-three days in the Manning Depot a group of twenty-four of us, all potential aircrew candidates, were called out and informed we were moving out. We went through the service drill of being "cleared" from the depot, which included turning in our bedding, etc. We boarded a chartered bus with an NCO in charge of the group. He informed us were being posted to No.7 Bombing and Gunnery School (B&GS) at Paulson, Manitoba, on what was termed "tarmac duty." Few, if any, of us had any idea of where Paulson was.

CHAPTER 2

Tarmac Duty

Paulson, it turned out, was nothing more than a siding east of Dauphin, near the shore of Dauphin Lake which served the school as a location for targets for practice bombing and a safe area for air-to-air machine gun firing. But this we were to learn later. Meanwhile, we had an enjoyable bus ride from Brandon via the summer resort area of Clear Lake where the bus stopped so we could stretch our legs and patronize a food outlet that served soft drinks and ice cream.

On arrival at 7 B&G we were put under the charge of a Flight Sergeant from Maintenance who ushered us through stores to draw our bedding and showed us to our quarters in one of the wartime barrack blocks. It was soon clear to us that tarmac duty consisted of what the service termed "joe jobs" such as sweeping hangar floors and cleaning washrooms and latrines. We didn't mind because we had heard horror stories of aircrew AC2s who had been sent to other units on guard duty, patrolling airfield perimeters at all hours of the day and night. But best of all, we were close to aircraft, the Fairey Battles and Westland Lysanders with which the station was equipped. We were free to clamber into them and inspect what seemed to us their massive arrays of instruments and controls, still mysteries to us.

One day our Flight Sergeant assigned some of us to clean latrines with the incentive that whomever he judged to have done the best job would get a "flip" in one of the aircraft. I was the winner and after donning harnesses for chest-pack parachutes the Flight Sergeant and I clambered into a Fairey Battle which was to be air tested.

The Battle was a Merlin-engined low-wing monoplane which had been proven obsolete in its intended role as a bomber. During the Battle of France in 1940, the squadrons equipped with The Fairey Battle suffered terrible losses at the hands of the Luftwaffe. It was designed to carry a crew of three—pilot, gunner and bomb aimer—the last of whom presided over a bombsight mounted over a mid-ships hole in the belly. The gunner sat on a seat rather like a piano stool, facing aft. The aircraft's coupe top of perspex ran from the pilot's windscreen along the fuselage, its last section covering the gunner when closed. This last section swung down and forward so, when opened fully, half of its length went down inside the coupe top while the other half projected upwards at about a 45-degree angle to form a windscreen for the gunner. When we boarded the aircraft, we stowed our parachute packs. The Flight Sergeant took over the gunner's seat facing aft while I stood up behind his back, my hands on each side of the cockpit and my body stooped inside the slanting perspex of the gunner's windscreen. Neither of us had helmets or any means of communication with the pilot, nor he with us.

The flight began marvellously and I thrilled as the Merlin, with its characteristic sound, tugged the heavy airframe along the runway and into the air. For me the perspective was unique, looking back over the tail and past the big rudder as they seemed to perform strange gyrations in relation to the earth, sky and horizon. I was enjoying the ride immensely when suddenly the tail dipped below the horizon, farther and farther, until it seemed that I was staring straight down at the earth. Then the aircraft began to drop out from under me as the pilot let the nose drop in a hammer stall. I clutched frantically at the cockpit rim as my feet left the floor and I started to part company with the airplane. My back rose into the angled canopy forming the wind-screen and I curved it in an attempt to wrap my tail bone around the locking bar that extended from side to side inside the perspex. I managed to get the small of my back up against the bar and stuck out my rear as far as I could to gain purchase on it. Then I held on, literally, for dear life.

In a moment the earth I had watched past the tail was replaced by sky as the aircraft stood on its nose. Then I was dropped out of the canopy to the floor and my knees buckled from the G-force as the pilot pulled the aircraft out of the ensuing dive. But at least I was now safely anchored to the floor. I swear if that antique airframe could be found today it would still bear the marks of my fingernails in the metal of the cockpit rim! It was my second flight in an RCAF aircraft and had it not been for that locking bar, it would have been my last.

Many of the staff pilots at the school were bored stiff with their occupation, having joined the air force to get into the war in the air. Some found relief by defying regulations and indulging in such forbidden practices as low flying. I recall two incidents that occurred during our stay at 7 B&G, both of which turned out unhappily for the pilots involved.

In one, the pilot decided to frighten some golfers on the course at Clear Lake and he swooped down on them so low that they dropped prone on the ground. Unknown to the pilot was the fact that one of the golfers was the Air Officer Commanding from Winnipeg who had the presence of mind to note the identification letters of the aircraft. A phone call to the Commanding Officer of the school terminated that pilot's career.

In another incident a pilot who had indulged in the forbidden sport landed believing he was home free. A short time later the SPs were looking for him. It turned out he had done his low flying over a ripened wheat field and when the ground crew checked the aircraft after the flight they found its tail well filled with wheat which the propeller had threshed and blown in to the bombsight hole in the belly of the aircraft!

As we became more familiar with the aircraft we were allotted minor tasks such as assisting with the starting of Battle engines. Our function was to tow a "trolley-ac" under the airplane and plug it into a receptacle on the underside of the fuselage. The trolley-ac consisted of a small gasoline engine, a generator and "accumulators" (what we would have called batteries) mounted on a small rubber-tired cart. Its purpose was to provide power to the aircraft's electrical system for starting thus eliminating the drain on the aircraft's internal batteries.

For the Fairey Battle there was only one correct way to do this. One backed up while stooping under the nose of the airplane from the front, past the wicked 14-foot metal propeller, plugged in and waited until the engine started. The trolley-ac lead then was unplugged and its airman attendant backed out from under the airplane to the rear, towing the cart and emerging under the trailing edge of one of the wings. We were told that not long before our arrival an airman had got the drill reversed. That is, he went under the airplane from the rear and then backed out to the front under the engine. The propeller decapitated him.

But our stint at 7 B&G was not all joe jobs. In our off-duty hours we were free to participate in the station's few recreation facilities. For some of us the best place to spend our evenings was in the WD's (airwomen's) canteen. It had a jukebox and girls to dance with. To this day if I hear "I've Got Spurs that Jingle, Jangle, Jingle" I am transported back in time to the happy evenings in that canteen. Here, too, the girls were allowed to wear clothing other than their uniforms thus diminishing somewhat the military ambience in which we spent our days.

And it was here my sex education was advanced a pace. One evening I noticed a particularly attractive girl sitting with an older airwoman. I approached the younger one and asked her to dance. She looked at her companion who shook her head negatively and emphatically. The girl declined my request. A short time later while dancing with another airwoman I was informed that the older of the two I had approached was a lesbian. That was the first time I recall having heard the word and my dance partner informed me the older one was "in love" with the girl I had asked to dance.

Thoughts of the girlfriends we had left at home led us into another pursuit, a form of jewellery making. Pieces of broken perspex were salvaged from the trash and cut into various shapes, mostly of the heart variety. After initial shaping these were polished for countless hours with a mixture of button polish and jewellers' rouge until a smooth and glossy finish was obtained. A small hole was drilled in the appropriate location into which a ring could be placed to form a sparkling pendant. Often a miniature in metal and enamel of the air force badge was affixed. It was not unusual to see three or four airmen sitting together on lower bunks involved in conversation, all with their fingers working constantly at polishing the bits of perspex. Probably hundreds of these creations were given to sweethearts and wives during the course of the war, and many are likely still in existence.

At Paulson, too, we were introduced to the military art of "swinging the lead." Another airman named Tucker and I were hangar sweepers together and on many bright sunny days the need for floor sweeping was minimal. We would do what was necessary and by early afternoon would find time hanging heavy on our hands. How we cottoned onto the drill, I can't remember, but we soon learned that if we strode through the guard house at the gate with bathing suits rolled in towels under our arms and, without stopping, barked "Night maintenance," in the general direction of the service policemen, they ignored us. As a result we spent several afternoons lounging on the beach.

One afternoon we arrived at the beach to find a car parked there—most unusual in days of wartime gas rationing. We continued on to the beach and were greeted with startled cries as three girls who had either been skinny dipping or sunbathing in the nude leaped up, gathered towels around them and fled to the shelter of their car. As I recall their naked forms were lovely.

At this time, too, the shortage of manpower on the prairies prompted the Service to grant "harvest leave" to non-essential personnel whose families could use their help on their farms. My father, in addition to being a businessman in our home village, also farmed a section and a half devoted, during the war, principally to the growing of flax. In August I applied for and was granted ten days' harvest leave. I made my way by train to Saskatoon where I was met by my father who drove me and my girlfriend to our hometown of Dinsmore. At this time my girlfriend was "marking time," waiting to enter the nurses' training program at Saskatoon City Hospital.

The next few days were idyllic. During the day, I drove a truck hauling flax to the village elevators and after sundown and the end of the day's harvest operations, spending the evenings with my sweetheart.

Too soon, my leave was over, but fate intervened in the form of a terrific thunderstorm the night before I was to be driven back to Saskatoon to catch the train to Paulson. My father made a valiant effort to get me to the city but we were only five or six miles from Dinsmore when it became apparent that the muddy prairie roads were impassable. We returned to Dinsmore and I sent a telegram to 7 B&G explaining my plight. The next day the roads had dried sufficiently that we were able to make it to Saskatoon and I returned to Paulson one day late.

The day after my return I was called in by the Flight Sergeant who waved some papers at me and informed me I had been put on charge for being AWL (Absent Without Leave) or, as we termed it, "A-W-Loose." He quizzed me on the circumstances and asked if I had notified the station about the rainstorm and road impassability. When

I told him I had, he barked a terse, "Come with me," and marched me to the Station Warrant Officer's office.

Our experience to that time as AC2s had instilled in us the belief that, insofar as other ranks were concerned, the SWO ranked second only to God. It was with great astonishment, therefore, that I heard the Flight Sergeant verbally tear into the SWO, demanding to know why one of his men had been put on charge without his having been consulted. After a short verbal tussle between the two in which the SWO definitely came out second best, the Flight Sergeant folded the charge papers several times and—Bang! Bang! Bang!—ran along their length with a stapler on the SWO's desk, then tossed them into the waste paper basket. He indicated to me that I should make myself scarce which I promptly did, utterly amazed that anyone dared to defy the SWO. I departed the office with a still-unblemished record! A day or two later, on 28 August, our group left 7 B&G having been posted to No.7 Initial Training School (ITS) in Saskatoon.

CHAPTER 3

Initial Training School

Our journey to Saskatoon from Paulson was a memorable one, taking almost twenty-four hours on what I am sure was the slowest train in western Canada. The coach in which we travelled was a veritable antique, probably one of the old colonist cars used by the railroads during the settlement of the West. The seats were hard and uncomfortable, but they could be transformed into lower berths and we were able to open the upper berths. There were no mattresses. We spent a very uncomfortable night sleeping in our greatcoats as the train made its slow way across western Manitoba and eastern Saskatchewan.

Sometime during the morning the train stopped at a prairie village and we were told it would be there for twenty minutes. Most of us dashed to a Chinese restaurant in the village and bought chocolate bars and soft drinks to assuage the pangs of hunger. Most of us made it back to the train. Several of the group, however, were still in the restaurant when the train pulled out without any prior warning. Those few were left in the village "improperly dressed" as most had left their caps and tunics on the train.

On arrival in Saskatoon we who had caught the train gathered up the effects of our unlucky comrades and were transported to the ITS which was located in what had been a Normal School on Avenue A (now Idlewyld Drive) close to what then was the northern edge of the city.

Our missing comrades arrived the next day and were promptly put on charge for being absent without leave, improperly dressed, and so on. But the miscreants were strangely unaffected by their fate. As it happened, the residents of the village had taken them in, fed them, gave them beds and even held a dance in their honour. In short, they had had a ball!

Our course consisted of 119 men and a group of us was quartered in the basement at the south end of the former Normal School building in a room that would have comfortably accommodated about one-half the number of double-tiered bunks with which it was equipped. This was our home, study area and bedroom for the ten weeks of our training.

ITS was the beginning of our careers as aircrew and we underwent an intensive ground school course. We were initiated into the mysteries of Theory of Flight, Airmanship, Navigation, Meteorology, Air Force Law, Armaments, Aircraft Recognition and hour after hour of Morse Code at which we were expected to attain a receiving proficiency of twelve words per minute on simulated radio signals and four words per minute on Aldis lamp. Our knowledge of mathematics was also brushed up.

The dedication which most of us devoted to the studies has always amazed me. Many of the members of our flight were former university students and I am sure none of them, including myself, had devoted nearly as much effort to their former studies as to these. It was here that the dreaded term "washed out" first entered our vocabulary and all were determined that it would not apply to them.

Here, too, we had our first encounter with the Link trainer. Those at the ITS were of a very basic type, with open "cockpits," limited instrumentation and, I suspect, were intended more to test our hand-foot-eye co-ordination than to make any valid assessment of our future flying ability. Just sitting at the controls of anything simulating an aircraft was a great thrill for us.

Our classes were held in what had been one of the city's collegiates, taken over by the RCAF "for the duration." This meant that each day we paraded south on Avenue A before turning west to the collegiate. We enjoyed these marches in the bright autumn days, accompanied by a single drummer whose monotonous rat-a-tat, rat-a-tat, rat-a-tat-tat-tat would occasionally be enlivened by a series of "hot licks" in jazz rhythms. And almost invariably we would be given an "Eyes right!" or "Eyes Left" when meeting pretty girls walking on the sidewalk. Some of them reacted haughtily with their eyes averted, quickening their pace to get by in a hurry, while others rewarded us with a smile and a wave of the hand.

In the collegiate there was a coke machine. What made this memorable was that during our time at ITS the price of a 6 ounce bottle of coke was raised from 5 to 6 cents. As the vending company had neither the means nor manpower to alter the machine, it overcame this problem by leaving every sixth bottle space in the machine empty. This meant that during our break periods we would stand around waiting for someone to put his nickel in and get nothing. There then would be an immediate rush until five bottles had been dispensed after which those who had not yet got their drink would stand around, casually unconcerned, waiting for another victim.

In addition to classes, there was a quite rigorous physical training program and I believe that by the time we had finished ITS most of us were in the best physical shape of our lives. We would go through a session of "physical jerks," then an obstacle course and wind up with four laps around a 440-yard cinder track and not even be breathing hard. But there was a hazard involved. An open area to the east of the normal school had been set aside for this training and had been mowed so the prairie growth was only two or three inches high. Unfortunately, most of this growth was Russian thistle which, in the autumn, was hard and thorny.

One day while playing touch football clad in baggy issue cotton shorts one member of our flight fell and slid on his rump for three or four feet through this growth. We escorted him back to our quarters where he lay face down across a bunk while three or four of us pulled dozens of thistle barbs out of his thighs and backside.

An unforgettable memory of 7 ITS in the fall of 1942 was the food in the Airmen's Mess. It was terrible. When marched back from the collegiate at lunchtime, we were paraded to the Mess and were supposed to march in single file through the door. Many of us would peel off before entering the Mess and make our way to the airmen's canteen where we could purchase a small, commercially-baked fruit pie, a half-brick of ice cream and a soft drink for twenty-five cents. I don't know how many of us subsisted for most of our initial training on this diet, supplemented with chocolate bars and the occasional weekend meal at one of the city's restaurants.

Then came the day of the turkey feast. Apparently word of the unsatisfactory food had got to Training Command Headquarters (HQ), and they sent an inspection team to investigate. As usual we were paraded to the Mess but this time were told that no one was to fall out. In the Mess we were served a superb turkey dinner—and not just at the usual steam table line-up, but on huge platters of carved turkey placed on the dining tables! Up to this time, we were unaware of the inspection and had we known of it the result might have been different but, needless to say, when the Orderly Officer arrived and the Orderly Sergeant called, "Any complaints?" the reply was silence. I don't remember that the food was any better after the inspection than it had been before.

While at ITS the change of seasons put us into "blues" and for the first time for most of us, we wore the famous "Air Force Blue" and were rid of the hated KD's, the khaki drill uniforms we had worn since entering the Manning Depot. This change brought a bonanza to the city's tailors because most of us had the uniforms altered to fit better. Many, too, had the narrow legs of the trousers widened by having the tailors add a wedge of material down the inside seam of the trouser leg. If detected, this practice was a cause for "disciplinary action."

The most significant addition to our dress at ITS was the white flash. This was a half-moon-shaped piece of a ribbed white material about five inches long which was inserted behind the band at the front of the wedge cap and showed above it. This flash signified that we were aircrew trainees. We were intensely proud to wear it.

During our stay at ITS there was a national Victory Loan campaign. As a promotion, it had been decided to stage a fake Nazi invasion of Saskatoon that would be defeated by units of the Canadian Army. We trainees at the ITS were to be the invading troops. We were issued black coveralls and equipped with the ubiquitous Springfield rifles and bayonets. Also, we each received two or three rounds of blank ammunition. This was done by lining us up and parading us past an NCO who handed each of us our ammunition ration. We soon discovered that merely by going around and rejoining the line we could garner a double issue, which several of us did.

We were loaded into trucks and taken to several key points in the city which the invaders were supposed to have taken. The group I was with was taken to the telephone exchange with instructions that we were to wait until a Canadian Army unit arrived, at which time we would fire our blank ammunition in a simulated battle before surrendering to the army and being paraded through downtown Saskatoon as the defeated enemy. Something went wrong with the plan.

After an enjoyable hour or two chatting with the girls in the telephone exchange, we began to wonder when the army would arrive. We waited, and waited, and waited. No Canadian Army. Having been informed of the timetable for the parade, we soon realized that somehow we had been forgotten. At this juncture an elderly private in the uniform of the Canadian equivalent of the Home Guard appeared walking down the street with his wife and a small child. He was dragooned into taking our surrender, equipped with one of our rifles and asked to escort us to Second Avenue to join the parade, which he did although somewhat reluctantly. Our timing was good and we tacked our group onto the parade of captured "enemy" soldiers being escorted by army units. However, we had not been disarmed nor had we used our blank ammunition so the citizens of Saskatoon were treated to the sight of defeated enemy soldiers gaily firing fusillades in all directions under the noses of their captors.

One scarcely expects a church parade to be a dangerous occupation but I nearly managed to get myself killed or severely injured one Sunday morning. The Protestant church service was held in the auditorium of the Normal School. We were paraded in, with the ground floor being filled first and with the remainder of us in the balcony. I, with several members of my course, wound up in the front row of the balcony with many of the school's staff airmen in the row behind us. At one point in the service when we were standing, the chaplain intoned, "Let us pray." I, with all of the others, tilted my head forward and closed my eyes. The next thing I remember is coming to on the floor between the seats and the balcony railing. Apparently, when I had inclined my head I had not stopped "inclining" and was about to go over the balcony railing when a staff airman grabbed my tunic belt and guided me to the floor. It was the only time in my life I have fainted and it was certainly a kind fate which had put an airman friend from my hometown directly behind me. The moral of the story is: "Don't skip breakfast when you are going on parade-even a church parade."

We didn't often discuss religion at any time in my service life but one night, after lights out, one of our course members made some comment about getting up for early Mass. This led to a discussion among many members of the course of the advantages and disadvantages of membership in various faiths, a discussion which became more and more spirited and which went on until the small hours. I don't believe anything much was resolved but it was clear that the majority involved was Protestant. But I recall the conclusion of the argument. The chap who had mentioned going to early Mass had the final word with, "If I die and go to heaven and you guys are there, I'm sure going to be mad!"

One source of great happiness for me in having been posted to 7 ITS in Saskatoon was that my girlfriend now was in training at Saskatoon City Hospital and so we were able to meet often. Although we were both confined to rigid hours, hers were far more restrictive. She had to be back in the nurses' residence by 10 p.m. most evenings with one or two "late leaves" each month when she was allowed to stay out until 11 p.m. However, we were able to enjoy early evening movies together, often with time for a snack at one of the local eating places, such as Picardy's, and a hug and kiss at the door of the residence before saying good night. We were much in love, with the intensity of emotion only eighteen-year-olds can experience. These evenings ended with me making my lonely way westward across the lines of railroad tracks which bisected the city, often having to climb over or duck under the couplers of strings of box cars, crossing a big vacant area south of a flour mill and thence to the grounds of the Normal School. These were surrounded by a high chain-link fence topped with several strands of barbed wire so one had to walk an additional couple of hundred yards to the Avenue A side on the west to gain entrance.

The final nerve-wracking ordeal at ITS was an aircrew medical examination. We all went into it praying that nothing of a medical nature would be found that would bar our continued training. Although I had gained a little weight since joining up, I was still underweight for my height. However, the medic who examined me merely commented that I would probably wind up on fighters as he thought I was too light to handle the heavies. I left the examination walking on air with visions of Spitfires dancing before me.

After what seemed like an amazingly swift passage of ten weeks, we graduated from ITS. This event was celebrated by a party at a downtown hotel the evening before our graduation parade. One member of our course had not only imbibed freely at the party, he had smuggled a bottle of whisky into the quarters from which he partook at frequent intervals during the night. He was in very shaky condition when we turned out for our graduation parade in the morning.

We attempted to conceal his condition by placing him in the middle of the centre rank of our flight and we pulled and pushed him through the sizing drill. He fitted this position quite naturally because he was one of the shortest men in the course. Somehow he got through this drill and roll call without attracting notice and the rest of us relaxed somewhat as we stood "at ease", awaiting the arrival of the CO. At this juncture, the SWO detected some movement in the flight behind us and bellowed, "Steady in number two!"

From the centre rank of our flight came an answering if somewhat drunken bellow, "Shteady in nummer two bu' not in nummer one!"

Our inebriated friend was immediately taken into custody and marched off of the parade ground under escort. It was just at this moment that the CO's party approached the parade ground from the opposite direction. Breaking away from his escort our friend staggered up to the CO, came to a tipsy attention directly in front of him and with an exaggerated salute offered a slurred, "Good Mornin', Shir." I never saw him again.

Graduation from ITS marked the first step upward in our service careers. We were reclassified from AC2 to Leading Aircraftman (LAC) and had the silvery cloth propeller denoting our new status sewn on the sleeves of our tunics approximately half way between elbow and shoulder. We wore them proudly even though, being a reclassification, it was not considered a promotion by the Service. But it did mean an extra twenty cents a day in pay boosting it to $1.35 which would be supplemented by 75 cents a day in flying pay when we started flying.

ITS ended with our postings to Elementary Flying Training Schools (EFTS) being announced. The group with which I had been associated since Manning Depot was scattered among several flying schools. As a result, I was separated from many good friends I had made up to this point in our service, particularly a group who had enlisted from United College in Winnipeg. Happily, some of us would meet again in the future.

CHAPTER 4

Elementary Flying Training School

When we arrived at 6 EFTS at Prince Albert we discovered the station was being operated by a civilian firm, the Northern Saskatchewan Flying Training School Limited, and our instructors consisted of a mix of civilian and RCAF pilots. But most delightful was our first experience with the airmen's mess. We could hardly believe our eyes.

We sat down to tables with place settings, had table service by young waitresses and a menu from which to choose. At breakfast, there were single-serving boxes of popular dry cereals and again, a choice of foods ranging from bacon and eggs to sausages and pancakes. We felt like royalty and decided that we really were going to enjoy being aircrew trainees if this was the sort of treatment we were to get all the way through. Little did we know that a far different regime would be in force before we left the unit.

I believe I was very fortunate in the instructor to whom I was assigned. He was a civilian—thorough, patient, friendly, and unlike at least one other instructor I encountered, never raised his voice beyond a level made necessary by the Gosport speaking-tube intercom system of the Tiger Moth. His name was D.P. Unwin and he had been flying since the year I was born. He was a man of middle height who, since we did all of our EFTS training in the winter, consistently wore a dark brown, furry inner flying suit without the accompanying coverall. This suit gave him the appearance of a big teddy bear. To top it all off he had a good sense of humour and we got along very well.

My first flight with Unwin was on 9 November 1942 and consisted mostly of familiarization with the aircraft, the airfield and the surrounding area. It lasted one hour and after it was over I felt almost as if I could fly without an airplane, so thrilled was I. The flights over the next ten days or so consisted mostly of "circuits and bumps," that is taking off, doing a circuit to the left around the airfield to the downwind side, and landing into wind. These flights ranged from fifteen to forty-five minutes in duration. Three or four times on longer flights of up to an hour and twenty minutes, I was initiated into basic safety procedures such as recovering from spins.

In ground school I and my fellow students were initiated into the mechanical systems of the Tiger Moth, such as brakes, the petrol system, operational limits of the Gypsy Major engine and so on, winding up with us signing certificates that we had received this instruction and also that we had read and understood Station Flying Orders. This done, we were eligible to fly solo whenever our instructors deemed us ready.

By 21 November I had logged eight hours and thirty-five minutes dual and was becoming envious of some of my fellow students who had soloed already. On that date I was disappointed when called out by Mr. Unwin for dual in Tiger Moth 4037. The reason for my despondency was that 4037 was equipped with skis and Station Flying Orders stated all first solo flights were to be made on wheel-equipped aircraft so the student had the benefit of brakes. At that time the field was covered with snow which was rolled and packed so aircraft with either wheels or skis could operate.

We did circuits and bumps for an hour and 5 minutes. As we turned at the upwind end of the field after one landing, Mr. Unwin told me to stop. He undid his safety harness, climbed out of the airplane and with a casual wave of his hand, said, "Away you go. One circuit." I was taken completely by surprise but didn't hesitate to taxi to the downwind end of the field, turn into wind and open the throttle. In a moment I was airborne and climbing away, somewhat shaken by the realization that the cockpit in front of me was empty, but I was elated beyond measure. I toyed for a moment with the idea of flying off for a few minutes, but reason prevailed and I stayed in the circuit.

Normally a circuit in the Tiger Moth was made in ten to twelve minutes but I managed to stretch it to twenty. It was probably the widest circuit the control tower had seen! I have been curious ever since to know how many trainees were permitted to do their first solo on skis.

Skis could be an embarrassment, particularly under conditions of strong wind. On one occasion when a particularly strong wind had come up suddenly, I landed, taxied up fairly close to the upwind end of the field and started to turn so as to taxi to the flight line at the hangar. The aircraft refused to turn. I gave it a strong blast of throttle with full rudder and it started turning but as soon as I eased off on the RPMs it weathercocked into wind again. This continued until the nose of the airplane was getting dangerously close to the airport fence at which point I gave up trying and sat in frustration and shame until a couple of ground crew men came out and manually turned the aircraft around. My only consolation was that I was not the only one to whom it had happened that day.

We learned soon that skis could definitely assist in making smooth landings. The front ends of the skis were tethered to the aircraft by bungee cords so when airborne they were tilted quite sharply upward. This meant that when landing, if one rounded out a few feet above the ground and let the aircraft settle slowly with some throttle on, one could feel the vibration when the back ends of the skis were on the ground. This was the signal to cut the power and the aircraft would settle smoothly onto the hard-packed snow.

Talk in the barracks was always of flying, with those of us whose instructors had not yet reached certain points in our training listening avidly to the accounts of those who had done things we had not. Often, on solo flights after one of these sessions, we who were behind would be tempted to try some of the manoeuvres described to us by others. This led to an encounter with my instructor at which, fortunately, he had the good humour to laugh.

The occasion was a check flight with an instructor acting for the Chief Flying Instructor. The check went well and I managed to perform everything asked of me without difficulty. After landing, I encountered Mr. Unwin in the hangar. He looked at me with raised eyebrow and inquired, "Who taught you to do slow rolls?" Then he smiled and walked away. Afterwards he did instruct me in slow rolls which led to a rather frustrating flight when we were doing dual aerobatics.

First, he had me do a couple of slow rolls to the left which were adequately performed. Then he told me to do a slow roll to the right. I began by putting the nose down and applying hard right aileron while moving the stick back. The airplane went up on its side and then the nose dropped uncontrollably in spite of my application of full top rudder. We wound up in a steep dive from which I resumed level flight. He told me to try it again. I did with the same result.

"I have control," he said into the Gosport and I released the controls. He began a roll to the right and got the same result I had so that exercise was abandoned. After we had landed I stowed my flight gear and after a few minutes walked out into the hangar. There I saw Mr. Unwin eyeing the airplane we had been flying. At last he walked behind the ship and sighted over the rudder along the fuselage. After a moment's contemplation he put his knee against one of the rudder hinges and, grasping the top of the rudder, bent it toward him. Again he sighted over the rudder and with a nod of satisfaction looked at me and said, "There. The damn thing will roll to the right now!"

As the surrounding countryside was snow covered, our cross-country flights and some others, such as practice forced landings, were done on ski-equipped aircraft. When doing practice forced landings flying orders stated we were not to go below 200 feet. The usual drill was that sometime during an instructional flight, the instructor would suddenly close the throttle and say, "Forced landing." It was up to the student to note the wind direction and select a field he thought he could get into without benefit of power. He then manoeuvred the aircraft to a position in relation to the field where, when down to about 200 feet, the instructor could assess whether or not a safe landing could be made. At this point he would tell the student to open the throttle and climb away.

During the descent the engine had to be revved up occasionally because the Gypsy Major, being air-cooled, could chill to the point where it would cut out, thus making a real forced landing necessary, accompanied by a severe dressing-down from the instructor. I never had it happen.

During one instructional flight Mr. Unwin cut the throttle, said "Forced landing," and then added, pointing, "The field behind that farm yard." I was a bit taken aback but proceeded to get into position. We got down to about 200 feet. He said nothing. We continued to descend until approaching the fence surrounding the field when he said, "I have control," and landed in the field. He taxied up to the farm yard, undid his harness and parachute and climbed out. I was left wide-eyed in the idling aircraft as he made his way to the farm house. In only a couple of minutes he returned, carrying a paper bag of eggs to take home to his wife!

The snow was deep and soft enough that although the main skis stayed on top the small tail-wheel ski had settled into the snow until the elevators were almost touching the surface. It took Unwin considerable jockeying of throttle, elevator and rudder to get the tail free, but it finally came loose and with the tail high he taxied quickly to the downwind end of the field, made a sweeping turn and took off. I couldn't help wondering what punishment would be inflicted on an instructor who got an aircraft bogged down in a snow-filled farm field on a practice forced landing.

During the first half of our course we lost a few of our companions whose instructors had decided they would not become satisfactory pilots. The fear of "washing out" was with us always. This led us to dub the really easy-to-fly Tiger Moth as the "Tigerschmitt," the "Washing Machine" or the "Maytag Messerschmitt." Happily, most of us made it through elementary flying training.

Early in December our civilian instructors disappeared for nearly two weeks. This was the prelude to the station being converted from a civilian-operated organization to an RCAF station. The most shattering aspect of this for us was the change in the airmen's mess. Gone were the place settings, menus, waitresses and nearly all of the niceties we had so appreciated when we had first arrived. In the mornings, instead of sitting comfortably at a table, contemplating whether we would have Corn Flakes or Rice Krispies for breakfast, we lined up at a steam table and took what the RCAF had to offer. On the whole the food was not bad, but the ambience of the airmen's mess changed beyond recognition.

The disappearance of our civilian instructors put us in the hands of RCAF pilots, none of whom were familiar to me. One I will never forget. On a day on which I was not scheduled to fly I went to the flight room in the hangar to bring my log book up to date. I had scarcely arrived when an unknown NCO instructor button-holed me and told me I was going flying with him. When I told him I had left my helmet my quarters, he cursed me up and down and opening a locker, took out a helmet and handed it to me.

I donned the helmet, which was about three sizes too big, along with my winter flying suit and accompanied him to an aircraft which I started up. I was told to taxi out to take off. According to him, everything I did was wrong from starting the engine to taxiing, each criticism buoyed along in a stream of profanity. He told me to take off and as soon as I opened the throttle my salvation occurred to me. He said something into the speaking tube which I couldn't hear over the roar of the engine because of the oversized loose-fitting helmet. Thereafter no matter how loudly he shouted, my constant reply to him was, "I can't hear you."

He continued shouting a stream of obscenities but I kept insisting I couldn't hear him so we were barely at circuit height when he told me to land. This I did, and apparently he didn't twig to the fact that I obviously had heard that. Even before I had shut down, he climbed out and stomped into the hangar. When I got into the flight room he was not visible so I stripped off my flying gear, replaced the helmet in the locker from which he had taken it and made myself scarce. Strangely, when I next went to make up my log book, there was no record of that flight so presumably he hadn't even bothered to sign out the aircraft. My only regret is not having any record of the s.o.b.'s name in my log book. I have no recollection of ever encountering him again, and I still feel sorry for the students who were regularly assigned to him.

There was one incident about which I still feel guilty. I was signed out for a solo flight and accompanied the ground crew man who would swing the prop out to the aircraft. I climbed in and we went through the starting drill. "Brakes on, gas on, throttle set, switches off," he called and I repeated each phrase after him. "Contact," he called after pulling the propeller through a couple of times and I turned on the two magneto switches and answered, "Contact." He swung the propeller and the engine caught, ran for a few moments and died.

"Switches off," he shouted and pulled the propeller through a couple of times again to prime the engine. "Contact," again. He swung the propeller with no result this time. This routine we had done two or three more times when glancing down, I noticed that I hadn't turned the gas on. I slowly sneaked the handle forward so as not to attract his attention to the moving lever on the carburettor which was visible to him through an opening in the engine cover if he happened to look. We went through the drill again and the engine roared into life, kept running and away I went.

The sequel to this incident came after the war. The ground crew man was a youth from my home town whom I had known most of my life. At a social gathering we were reminiscing about our experiences at Prince Albert and I confessed. At that distance in time, we were both able to laugh about it but at the time he probably would have wrung my neck gladly.

On all flights it was customary for the "first pilot" to check the aircraft's Form L-14 to ensure the aircraft had had its Daily Inspection (DI), was refuelled and OK'd by the various ground crew trades concerned with its maintenance. The first pilot then signed as having accepted the aircraft. On dual flights the instructor always was the first pilot.

Off one day on a dual instructional flight with Mr. Unwin, we were airborne and climbing away from the airport when I noticed that the floating pencil of the vertical gauge on the gas tank forming the centre section of the top wing was very close to the bottom. I got on the Gosport and informed Mr. Unwin. He replied that he was sure the L-14 had indicated the aircraft had been refuelled and opined that occasionally the floating pencil of the gas gauge stuck or froze down. We continued for a minute or two and then he said, "You have control," and cautioned me to keep the aircraft straight and level.

I watched with curiosity as he slid his coupe top back and undid his safety harness and parachute straps. My curiosity changed to astonishment when he stood up in his cockpit. I'm sure my eyes must have been as big as saucers and my grip on the stick vice-like when he grasped the centre section struts, stood on his seat and placing one foot on each edge of the cockpit, reached across to the leading edge and pulled himself up so he was lying on his chest on the top wing, buffeted by the 110-mile-an-hour slipstream at something like 30 degrees below zero Fahrenheit. Unscrewing its cap, he peered into the gas tank. He replaced the cap, allowed himself to slide backwards, dropped into his seat and announced to me that we were nearly out of gas. We landed and taxied to the hangar line without the engine quitting. But nothing can describe the sensation felt by a student pilot with fifteen or twenty hours' total flying time, straining to ensure that the aircraft didn't so much as waver in its attitude, while he watched his instructor performing such a feat—without his parachute.

Ground school at the EFTS was not nearly as intensive as at ITS. The main emphasis was on navigation, airmanship and aircraft recognition. One interesting diversion was added as part of our armaments training. This was indoor skeet shooting.

Large sheets of white cloth draped one windowed wall of a hangar-like drill hall and extended at right angles to the wall a good portion of its width. The skeet were small, black, about two and one-half inches in diameter and extremely fragile. The "shotguns" were .22 calibre rifles, the shells filled with a very small quantity of lead shot not much coarser than dust and easily stopped by the cloth drapes. This was, for me, a continuation of the "deflection shooting" I had first encountered when duck hunting. Whether this was something added to the course by the civilian operators I don't know, but I never encountered .22 calibre shot shells anywhere else in the air force.

During the first two weeks in December I flew with an assortment of instructors, all RCAF, ranging in rank from Sergeant to Pilot Officer. Then, on 14 December my former instructor reappeared wearing the uniform and rank badges of a Sergeant pilot in the RCAF. From then on my log book lists several flights with Sergeant Unwin whereas before it had always been Mr. Unwin.

Quite honestly, I was shocked that an instructor of his experience and capability, when compared to some of the RCAF pilots I had flown with in the interim, was taken into the service at the lowest rank for the aircrew trades.

My first flight with Sergeant Unwin was a dual cross-country of an hour and thirty-five minutes duration on December 14. Before the end of the course I was to do three more, solo, all of just under two hours. Those were probably the longest two-hour periods of my flying career, not because of any difficulties with navigation, but because of the cold.

The air temperature at cruising height ranged anywhere from 30 to 50 degrees below zero Fahrenheit and the cockpit of the Tiger Moth was unheated. Under these conditions, keeping a pencilled log, handling maps for map reading and working a Dalton computer strapped to one thigh while attempting to keep the aircraft straight and level was anything but a pleasure. With gloves on it was impossible to make legible log entries and with them off, fingers were numb and insensitive almost immediately, and they soon became acutely painful. One's blood quickly stirred into vigorous action when one signed out to do practice aerobatics. The thrills of doing loops and rolls, stall turns and spins seemed to keep us warm. When doing spins, I liked to position myself over a crossroads, preferably with farm buildings in one corner so I could count the times the farm came around. And I found it entertaining when doing loops to look out directly to one side or the other to watch the horizon rotating 360 degrees past the interplane struts.

A solo aerobatics flight was almost the end for one of the members of our course. The Tiger Moth was an easily managed aircraft but it had one dangerous characteristic: it was difficult to get it to recover from an inverted spin and as a consequence we were warned against any manoeuvre which might get us into one. Further, we were told that if we did get into an inverted spin and hadn't recovered by the time we were down to a certain height, 3000 feet if I remember correctly, we should abandon the aircraft. The student, who could have lost his life, later told us excitedly of his adventure.

I believe he was doing stall turns when he somehow got the airplane spinning upside down. He narrated how he had tried everything he could think of to stop the spin without success and finally, when the altimeter indicated he was dropping past the critical altitude, he let go of everything to open the coupe top and bail out. When he released all of the controls, the aircraft came out of the spin by itself! He resettled himself in his seat and continued the flight. No one could offer any explanation for what had happened, but the incident certainly reinforced our faith in the aircraft.

From 18 to 23 December I was initiated into night flying. This phase of the course consisted almost entirely of circuits but it was exciting to take off along the line of smoky flare pots and to learn to judge one's height on landing by watching the flares seemingly approach one another as one descended.

More thrilling was the different aspect of the world with glittering stars above and bright lights on the ground reflecting from the snow-covered landscape, each individual light set in the centre of its own small circle of lighted snow.

Keeping watch for other aircraft at night was a far different problem than during daylight. The only indication of their presence was the bright red, green and white navigation lights and some practice was required to interpret from the lights their relative positions and courses in relation to one's own aircraft. My night flying training at EFTS totalled 4 hours and 15 minutes dual and 45 minutes solo. It never occurred to me at that stage that a large proportion of my subsequent training and operational flying would be done at night. After all, I was confident I was destined to fly fighters, most of which seldom flew at night.

The last week of our course was Christmas week. We were given Christmas Day off but flew on the 24th and 26th. In fact, flying seemed to intensify markedly during the last couple of weeks of the course, perhaps making up for the two weeks our civilian instructors had been missing. In the last six days I flew 26 hours and 15 minutes of the total of 70 hours I logged in our eight weeks at Elementary. This included the last day which was my longest with 4 hours and 45 minutes in the air on five separate flights along with two sessions in the Link trainer totalling 1 hour.

That week was notable for two other reasons. First, my girlfriend's nursing school gave her a weekend off on 19 and 20 December. On the 19th she arrived in Prince Albert by train and checked into a hotel. Although I was on duty on both of her days off, I was able to meet her in her hotel late in the afternoon of the 19th and we had dinner together in the hotel dining room. I had to be back on the station ridiculously early, but we had a few happy hours together during which I was able to give her the Christmas present I had bought for her, a cultured pearl necklace representing almost a month's pay.

The second notable event of the week, or rather series of events, began on Christmas Eve. We were to have Christmas Day off so several of us went into the town of Prince Albert for the evening. At one point, we were walking in twos and threes along a sidewalk bordered with pines. One of the pair walking in the lead was idly flicking the pine branches as he passed them. One of these, not anticipated, hit a following airman in the face and one eye. We learned later that he had two or three pieces of pine needle extracted from one eyeball, but happily his vision was not impaired. His name was Murray Fallow and I encountered him again after the war when he was Chief Flying Instructor with the Edmonton Flying Club. He checked me out on a Cessna 140.

The evening continued with the rest of us imbibing a little too freely with the result that while walking along a street lustily singing Christmas carols, we were picked up by the service police and herded into their van. A minute or two later the SPs spotted another character behaving inappropriately and stopped to gather him in as well. While doing this they left the back door of the van open and I saw the opportunity to make my escape from the clutches of the law. Unfortunately, I didn't make allowance for the slipperiness of my service boots on the icy street and after only a few steps, found myself flat on my back looking up at a very stern SP. I was herded back into the paddy wagon and we were all transported to the EFTS. However, in the spirit of Christmas, none of us was put on charge.

What has amazed me ever since is how I managed to get through all of this without the two bottles of beer I had in each greatcoat pocket being detected. I must have clanked like a freight train. As we returned to our barracks, I shoved the four bottles deep into a snowdrift near the door. The next morning, four of us breakfasted on a roast turkey and other goodies which my mother had mailed to me. I retrieved the beer from the snowbank to add to our repast but it was so cold that when we snapped the caps off, it froze solid! Later, we had another turkey dinner in the airmen's mess

It was during that last week of intensive flying that I came close to meeting my doom. When there was a wind change, it was signalled to aircraft in the air and on the ground by setting off smoke canisters at the upwind end of the field, the smoke streaking downwind in continuous dense clouds rising 30 or 40 feet above the ground. While the smoke was billowing along the ground, one was supposed to take off with the smoke on one's left and land with the smoke on one's right.

I was taking off under these conditions and was just nicely airborne when ahead of me and almost at right angles to my line of flight, another Tiger Moth emerged from the smoke at almost the same altitude. My reaction was pure reflex. I shoved the stick forward and almost immediately pulled it back as the other "kite" roared over my head. I am sure its wheels weren't more than 4 or 5 feet above my top wing when our paths crossed and that my wheels cleared the ground by not more than a foot or so. I would still like to know just what the hell they were doing, particularly as I saw an instructor in the front cockpit. I don't believe either the instructor or student saw me, but even today I just have to close my eyes and I can see that aircraft. I reported the incident after landing but never did learn the identity of the clot captaining the other plane

I finished EFTS the day before my nineteenth birthday with 70 hours in my log book, 65 day and 5 night, and was posted to No. 4 Service Flying Training School in Saskatoon. I had to report on 10 January 1943 after about ten days' leave. I spent most of my leave in Dinsmore, showing off my elevated status as a fledgling pilot by wearing my battledress in public (a no-no), flying boots (another no-no) and white silk scarf (a third no-no)!

CHAPTER 5

Service Flying Training School

I was somewhat ambivalent about my posting to 4 SFTS in Saskatoon. On the one hand, it put me close to my hometown and, more importantly to me, I would be able to see my girlfriend frequently. On the other hand, the school was flying twin-engined Cessna Cranes which did not augur well for my desire to become a fighter pilot. However, I consoled myself with the thought that there were twin-engined fighters such as the Bristol Beaufighter or, even more attractive, the superb new DeHavilland Mosquito.

I could not help but recall the situation a few months earlier when 4 SFTS had been equipped with North American Harvards which I, enthralled, had watched as they flew low across the northern part of the city, sweeping up and over the higher river bank on the south side with the bellowing roar of their engines shaking plates in the cupboards of Nutana residences. I was consoled somewhat by my instructor's assurance that if one could fly multi-engined aircraft, one could fly anything whereas those who trained on single engines could fly only single-engined planes.

Again I felt myself lucky in the instructor to whom I was assigned. He was Pilot Officer C.R. "Cec" Rain, a pleasant, even-tempered young officer with a broad streak of devilment in his character. These qualities made flying with him enjoyable—most of the time— with occasional moments of excitement and, occasionally, downright terror.

Our introduction to the Cessna Crane Mark I led us into new complications in flying. First, there were many new instruments to comprehend and, where the engines were concerned, two of everything. Next, the aircraft had flaps and retractable undercarriage, complete with warning horn which blasted your ears if you closed the throttles with the wheels up. It also had a complete blind flying panel of gyro instruments. Later, we were introduced to constant speed propellers on the Crane IA. At first it seemed to us that flying was getting very complicated but it was only a short time until we were completely accustomed to what had at first seemed to be a baffling array of new gadgetry.

Our time at SFTS was divided between flying and ground school. In the latter we spent what seemed like endless hours on classroom navigation exercises interspersed with classes on Airmanship, Armaments, Meteorology, Signals, Aircraft Recognition and Aircraft Engines. The instructor tasked with teaching us about engines was a Senior NCO whose basic attitude was, "What do you care about the guts of an engine as long as it runs?" As a result his classes were largely pleasant bull sessions which came as welcome breaks from the more rigorous attention required in most others.

He made himself the butt of most of his own yarns and amused us with tales of his past run-ins with the service police. It seems he had a tendency to partake too freely of alcoholic beverages when on leave or on a pass, which almost invariably landed him in the clutches of military law. During our time there, he decided to have a boozy weekend without any risk. The following Monday he came into class, threw his cap down disgustedly and told us his tale of woe.

He related that he had got a bottle of whisky and a hotel room. Friday evening, he locked himself in the room, threw the key through the transom and proceeded to do away with the whisky. Sunday morning, relatively sober and congratulating himself for staying out of trouble, he called the hotel desk, was liberated from his room and walked out the hotel door—where he was promptly picked up by the service police for walking out in public without a cap! We never knew whether or not his tales were true but he was a great entertainer.

My predominant memory of the first few weeks at SFTS is of the cold. We began our flying on 12 January 1943 and for the next month or so it seemed the temperature seldom rose above zero degrees, Fahrenheit. There was a period of about three weeks when the daily weather report posted in the flight room read simply "CAVU"- Ceiling and Visibility Unlimited. There were days on end when thermometers on the ground registered 20 and 30 degrees below zero and lower.

One morning P/O Rain and I were first off. We sat at the end of the take-off strip on the rolled snow field for 15 or 20 minutes waiting for the cylinder head temperatures to climb into the normal range, by which time we were nearly frozen. We took turns holding our hands over the cabin "heater," a pipe of about one-half-inch diameter which projected upward through the cabin floor between the pilots' seats and produced a barely detectable flow of slightly warmed air. Finally we got airborne but before we had climbed to 500 feet Rain said, "The hell with this!" He took control, did a very fast, very tight, very low circuit, landed and taxied at breakneck speed to our flight's hangar doors where he shut the engines down. We did no more flying that day.

The Jacobs air-cooled engines of the Crane were very sensitive to sub-zero cold in spite of the addition of winter fronts which covered about 80 percent of the area inside the ring of the cowling, limiting the air flow around the cylinders. This gave student pilots another unenviable chore.

First thing in the morning students not scheduled to fly immediately were detailed to climb into aircraft in the hangar. Each plane was pushed by the ground crew up to the doors which were then opened just enough to allow the plane through. As soon as the props were clear of the door line, the student hit the starter switches to get the engines running. If he tried more than once or twice without success, the aircraft was pushed aside because it froze up almost instantly. If the engines caught, the aircraft was taxied to the parking area on the tarmac and the student sat in it, shivering in the metal bucket seat until a student and instructor or a solo student came to take it over.

This frigid weather produced risks not associated with our duties. One night after attending a movie in the city with my girlfriend, I returned to the station by bus and was dropped at the guardhouse on the east side of the field. I walked to our barrack block which was located at the extreme southwest corner of the station's buildings. In defiance of a rigid prohibition against walking across the parade square, now snow-covered and unused, I took a chance and cut diagonally across it.

In seven or eight minutes I was at our barrack block and as I reached for the doorknob I heard a distinct "snap" which seemed to emanate from somewhere right in front of me. On entering the warmth of the block it wasn't long before I discovered, somewhat painfully, the origin of the sound. The tip of my nose had frozen audibly!

Much of our initial "circuits and bumps" flying was done from an alternate airfield at Vanscoy, near Saskatoon. This field had one hangar with a control tower on one corner and inside thirty or forty brand new Tiger Moths. These were packed into the hangar like sardines in a can. One had been pushed in and tilted up so it was standing on its wheels and nose, its tail high in the air. A second was then nested up against it in the same fashion and so on. We were told they had been built with Menasco engines as substitutes for the Gypsy Major but had proved so dangerously under-powered they were never used for training. What became of them, I don't know.

Flying instruction at SFTS was intensive. During the slightly less than four months on course there, I flew 138 times, not counting many flights as a "passenger," keeping lookout on the port side of the aircraft while an instructor gave instrument flying instruction to another student. The canvas wrap-around hood which blocked the student's view of the outside world also effectively blocked the instructor's ability to see anything to port of the aircraft so an additional pair of eyes on the left was essential. Often these flights would be of two or more hours duration, with two students taking turns at being lookout and receiving instruction. Each logging about one-half of the time as "dual."

The instruction ran the gamut of the aircraft's capabilities which did not include aerobatics. Initially it was concerned with the basics-rate 1 turns, steep turns, stall symptoms, fixed-rate climbs and descents with climbing and descending turns, precautionary take-offs and landings, map reading and cross-countries dual and solo. Later we did instrument and night flying cross-countries, and had plenty of solo time throughout to practice handling the aircraft in all types of manoeuvres. It was on one of these solo flights I almost met my destiny.

It was late in January or early in February when I took off under CAVU conditions to spend an hour or so practising steep turns. I flew to one of the solo flying areas southeast of Saskatoon and at about 5000 feet started my exercises, putting the aircraft into a steep turn one way or the other and going round and around and around, keeping the rate of turn constant without losing or gaining altitude. My attention was rivetted mostly on the horizon and the aircraft's instruments.

After three-quarters of an hour or so, I decided to return to the airport and I looked down. The ground was gone. There was nothing visible beneath me but a solid white blanket of blowing snow, gleaming white under the sun.

Knowing that most of the weather in that part of Canada moved from west to east, and well aware of the hazards of letting down under such conditions, I decided my best course of action was to head for the SFTS at Yorkton, about 200 miles to the southeast, hopefully getting there before the blowing snow arrived. As Yorkton was well outside the area covered by my local map, I reached for the envelope of emergency maps with which each aircraft was supposed to be equipped—only to discover there wasn't one!

While mentally cursing the clot who had removed the maps, I pondered my situation and decided I had two possible courses of action: I could either try to let down through the snow or I could bail out and let the aircraft go. Somehow, I couldn't bring myself to do the latter, not from fear but because I was sure it would mean the end of my flying career. I elected to let down. I put the aircraft into a shallow spiral descent and pressed my face up against the left side window to peer downward. About the time I was entering the top of the snow I glanced at my instruments and discovered my rate of turn and descent had increased dangerously. As I was flying a Crane IA with constant-speed propellers, there was no increase in engine RPM or sound to warn me that my rate of descent was increasing dangerously. From that moment on my eyes were constantly in motion, peering down out of the window and returning to the instruments.

As I continued to descend as slowly as possible I realized that spotting the snow-covered ground before I hit it was going to be a matter of luck. I was lucky. Suddenly a dark shape appeared off my port wing—a grain elevator. I levelled off perhaps 50 feet above the ground and circled the elevator. I knew that Saskatoon was known as the "Hub City" because nearly all of the railroads in that part of Saskatchewan radiated out from it like the spokes of a wheel so all I had to do was follow the railroad which served the elevator. The tracks were clearly visible from 50 feet or so up, the only black lines in an all-white landscape. But which way?

My descent through the snow had thoroughly disoriented me but I knew I had been southeast of Saskatoon so all I had to do was follow the railroad northwest. Which way was northwest? We had been told many times to trust our instruments so I lined up on the railroad with what my gyro direction indicator and compass told me was northwest. Every nerve in my body screamed that I was going the wrong direction but I decided to take the informed advice of our instructors and follow the instruments.

After only a few minutes of skimming along just over the telegraph poles beside the tracks I was suddenly confronted with a large black shape looming out of the snow directly ahead of me. I hauled back on the control column and zoomed over it while at the same time breathing a sigh of relief. I recognized the shape as the coaling tower in Sutherland, a small railroad town just outside of Saskatoon, and knew exactly where I was in relation to the airport.

Moments later I crossed the airport fence and made a flapless landing into the gale-force wind blowing from the west. The wind was so strong the aircraft didn't roll more than a few yards after touchdown. I taxied to our hangar where there were no aircraft on the line and an alert groundcrew type met me and waved me up to the hangar doors. I shut the engines down, went into the flight room through the hangar and stripped off my flying clothing. The portal was closed where our airwoman timekeeper usually sat so I rapped on the door of the room she shared with the instructors. A male voice told me to come in and I entered to find four instructors, not including my own, sitting at a table playing cards.

"What do you want?" the Flight Commander demanded.

"I want to sign in," I replied.

"Don't you know you are supposed to sign in as soon as you land?" he asked gruffly.

"I just landed," I said.

Four faces stared at me, wide-eyed. "Christ!" the OC blurted. "That damned timekeeper told me all of our air-craft were in! Where have you been?"

I related the tale of my experience and was dismissed with the comment that I was lucky to be alive, a comment with which I silently agreed.

Another of my instructional flights was a dual instrument cross-country with a turning point at a village named Conquest, about twenty miles by road from my home town, near which was located a dance barn I had attended often. What impressed me most was what a short flight it was from Saskatoon and a plan began to form in my mind for the future. It wasn't long before the plan was realized.

Signed out one day for solo practice flying, I headed for my home village, about sixty-five air miles southwest, and did a couple of tight circuits around it at well below the 200-foot minimum limit we were supposed to observe. What I didn't know was that the village had a new Roman Catholic priest, a hobby photographer, who had taken a photograph of my plane—which included a neighbour's car! The plane's identification number was clearly visible.

He had shown the picture to a few people and word of it got to a man who once had been fired by my father and who had always held a grudge against our family. He asked the priest for a copy but, fortunately for me, he was refused. I am sure it would have been in the hands of the RCAF station commander very quickly. When I was next home on a 48-hour pass, the priest gave me the only copy of the photo—and the negative.

Part of our training consisted of navigation exercises in Mk I Avro Ansons or "Flying Greenhouses" as we called them. In all, for me, these consisted of seven flights of up to 3 hours and 30 minutes' duration. Usually there were three students involved, one acting as second pilot (although we were not qualified on the type), one as first navigator and one as second navigator.

The honour of being second pilot was somewhat diminished by what seemed to be that person's principal duty—cranking up the kite's retractable undercarriage. This, as I recall, required 270 turns of a crank located between the two pilots' seats plus a considerable period of time and expenditure of muscle energy after getting airborne. We learned that the Anson was the first aircraft of the RAF to have a retractable undercarriage and we speculated that it was designed before the RAF had learned of the invention of the hydraulic pump.

My crowning achievement (or so I thought—for a time) in this series of exercises was a 3-plus-hours flight on which I was first navigator. After giving the pilot the course for the last leg of the flight I watched with great satisfaction as we approached the airport and noted that on ETA (Estimated Time of Arrival) we were almost directly over it. I began packing up my navigation gear and waited for the pilot to begin letting down to join the circuit. The plane continued straight and level.

After a minute or two I noticed the Flying Officer navigation instructor eyeing me quizzically. Finally, he asked sarcastically, "Don't you think you had better tell the pilot we have arrived?" It hadn't occurred to me such a thing would be necessary when on a perfectly clear, bright sunny day, the airport had been visible for the last ten minutes. Of course, the pilot and instructor were right and I had goofed.

One solo flight, known as a height test, was of special interest. On this exercise the student was told to take the aircraft as high as he could get it to go. I did the height test in a Crane IA and in approximately an hour was able to get it to between 12,000 and 13,000 feet. The interesting part was the reaction of the aircraft controls at that height. One could move the control column back and forth over a wide arc with little reaction by the aircraft other than an extremely mushy feeling. The ailerons reacted similarly. Altogether the sensation was rather as if the aircraft was wallowing, barely hanging onto its height, while mushing along at a fairly acute angle of attack. It felt as if the aircraft was going to drop out from under me at any moment.

In the sixth week of the course we began night flying which lasted for slightly more than one week during which I accumulated a little more than eighteen hours on nineteen flights. This total included three cross-countries totalling six hours. We were warned that night flying in the blackout conditions of Britain would be far more difficult than we were experiencing in Saskatchewan where there were lights everywhere.

In the event, a few months later I found the situation to be exactly the opposite. In Saskatchewan, the lights of every village looked much the same and it was difficult to tell one from another; in Britain the only lights visible were the so-called "occults" and "pundits" which flashed their identifying codes telling you exactly where you were—provided they weren't switched off because of enemy air activity.

Our night flying was done while the airfield was still snow-covered and the flare path was literally that—rows of flare pots set out on the packed snow. These pots were like over-sized, garden watering cans with a wick protruding from the snout and fuelled by kerosene. It was one of the duties of the student pilots to collect these when the night's flying activities ended.

My turn at this task was accomplished in company with three other students and a driver with a stake truck from which the sides had been removed. The driver drove at a reasonable pace along the line and a student on the running board scooped up each pot, passed it back to another who swung it up to be grabbed by a student on the truck deck where it was snuffed out with a cap attached to the pot by a chain. The deck of the truck soon was covered with spilled kerosene which, as one might expect, caught fire when a flare pot tipped before being extinguished. However, a couple of quick squirts with a CO_2 extinguisher soon had the flames out with no damage to the truck and we completed the task in the cold light of a wintry dawn.

There was a sequel to this episode. We had finished the task just in time to get to ground school without breakfast and were faced with a navigation examination. Our protests were ignored and the examination proceeded. Needless to say, our results were far from meeting the standard required and later the head navigation instructor let us know this in no uncertain terms. We were threatened with dire consequences—none of which came to pass as far as I can recall.

Instructional flying must have become very boring for our instructors so it is no wonder they occasionally broke the rules. Once, signed out for I don't recall what type of instruction, P/O Rain asked if it was true that my hometown was within easy flying distance. When I assured him it was, he told me to direct him to it. We circled the village a couple of times at a reasonable altitude and then he asked if there was a nearby farm we could "beat up" without being reported. I pointed one out to him, about a mile south of the town, which was farmed by a young couple with whom I was very friendly. He circled to the west and let down until we were skimming along only a few feet above a mile-wide stubble field and were headed straight for the farm house. It was his obvious intention to fly straight at the house and zoom up over it, clearing it by only a few feet.

We were almost at the point where he would have to pull up when we spotted the white decorative globes part way up the shafts of very tall lightning rods atop the house. Rain's reaction was almost instantaneous and later, on reflection, I had to admire the speed of his reflexes. He pulled back on the control column while simultaneously cranking on hard right aileron. The aircraft started to climb, banking steeply, and we went by the house, the port wing rising over the nearest lightning rod and the starboard wing dipping between the house and a garage about twenty feet from it. We climbed away safely, while he turned to look at me with a wide grin. If I grinned in return, it was probably a pretty shaky effort.

Near the end of March I was called out by Rain for a dual trip and was surprised to have a passenger with a large briefcase climb into the back seat. It turned out we were flying an accounts officer to the EFTS at Prince Albert. We landed there, dropped our passenger off at the hangar with the control tower, and taxied out to take off again.

The layout of the field at P.A. was like a reversed and inverted "L," with the hangars along the inside of the long arm of the L. Depending on the wind direction one took off and landed parallel to the hangars, or at right angles to their line on the crossbar of the L. On the day we were there, the latter was the case. Being familiar with the field I was somewhat puzzled when Rain taxied out on the area that was not in use and I was more than somewhat startled when he turned the aircraft into wind facing the hangar line and opened the throttles.

We roared straight across the area at 90 degrees to the normal direction in which it was used and, it seemed to me, without a hope of making it over the hangars. I was wrong, but just barely. When we were so close to the hangars I was sure we were going to plough straight into the side of one, he hauled back on the controls so sharply the tail wheel hit the ground. The aircraft literally jumped up about thirty feet and we roared across the flat roof of the hangar with the control tower on it, at just about eye level with the tower's occupants. I am willing to bet Rain never tried that again but he certainly scared the hell out of me, if not himself.

Except for the cold early in the course, we had almost perfect flying weather for most of the time. As a result we had all finished the instructional phases of the course nearly three weeks ahead of schedule. I took my Wings Test and Wings Instrument Test on 6 April and most of the other course members had theirs within a few days either way of that date. We weren't scheduled to graduate until 30 April. As a result, a large proportion of our flying time for the last three weeks consisted of what was known as mutual instruction, that is, two student pilots flying together sharing the time, and frequently just enjoying themselves.

It was on one of these flights another student and I almost qualified ourselves for "washing out." We were doing mutual instruction southwest of Saskatoon and decided to indulge in a little low flying. Pike Lake seemed to be a good spot. We went across the lake, which by this time was unfrozen, at nearly zero feet. As we approached the far shore a flock of ducks suddenly flew up in front of us. We pulled up sharply and managed to avoid them, thereby proving that a Cessna Crane could outclimb a duck, but we were grateful we hadn't collected one or two in our engines. That would have been difficult to explain.

On another of these flights a trainee by the name of Smoker and myself had landed and were taxiing in to park the aircraft with Smoker driving. As we swung into position in the circular pattern in which the aircraft were parked, our port wingtip made slight contact with the wingtip of an adjoining plane. On examination we found the green-tinted glass on the wingtip light of the other plane had been broken and we were positive we were finished as far as our flying careers were concerned; damaging an aircraft was almost always a one-way ticket down washout street.

We managed to make contact with the Senior NCO in charge of maintenance who agreed to have a look and decided that no other damage had been done to either aircraft. He said he would see that the broken wingtip light's glass was replaced and told us to forget it, so the mishap was never reported—for which we were truly grateful.

There was an incident on the ground during our course of rather a bizarre nature. On one pay parade we were addressed by the CO of the station who informed us there had been a shortage found in the station's Non-Public Funds and all station personnel were being docked a certain amount to make it up. The amount for each of us was trivial, around $2.00 as I recall but, quite naturally, we were unhappy about it. Evidently word of this reached someone higher up the chain of command and a few days later we were called out for a special pay parade at which we all got our money back. I never heard any further details of the incident but I assume some accounts type found himself in deep trouble. It was rumoured among us that a Link trainer instructor, a veteran of the Royal Flying Corps in World War I, had blown the whistle on the caper by calling Training Command HQ.

At last the day of our Wings Parade arrived. The preceding evening we celebrated at a Wings Party in the Bessborough Hotel in which we all booked rooms. My date was my girlfriend whose nursing authorities didn't see the need for any extension of her very restricted hours so I had to have her back at the nurses' residence by 11 p.m. Although the party continued well into the small hours of the morning we were all up and fit for the parade.

There was a Victory Bond drive on at the time and so, as a publici-ty-gaining measure, the parade was held in downtown Saskatoon in a park on the riverside adjoining the Bessborough. Those of us who had relatives close enough to attend were given the privilege of having someone close to us pin on our wings. As a result I was able to receive my wings from my father who, having already lost one son in the war, must have performed the task with mixed emotions. However, to me he displayed only pride at my accomplishment in having been given a "distinguished pass."

Following the ceremony we were transported back to the SFTS where we were paraded in a groundschool room and the list of those of us who had been awarded commissions was read out. I was fortunate enough to be one of them. We were dismissed and returned for the last time to our barrack block to collect our belongings before going on leave. Here one of our fellow graduates amused us with a confession.

Early in the course, when temperatures were sub-zero and the field snow-covered, he had finished a landing by standing a Crane vertically on its nose. At the time he maintained stoutly that the brakes had frozen, this in the face of declarations by all in authority that the brakes on the Crane never froze up. The next day the Chief Flying Instructor landed and promptly ground-looped. Cause? The brakes on one wheel had frozen. Our friend was off the hook. But after those coveted wings were firmly in place on his chest he admitted to us that he had been afraid of over-shooting and had applied the brakes so strongly that the aircraft had flipped up on its nose! I hope his luck continued to be as good.

Another not-quite-so-amusing incident for two of us occurred when many of us returned to our rooms in the Bessborough Hotel. Some, including me, had enlisted the hotel's valet service to sew sergeant's stripes on our tunics. I hurriedly removed my jacket from a closet and proceeded to cut the sergeant's stripes off. It was only after I had removed them from one sleeve and was turning the jacket over to get at the other that I realized it wasn't my tunic! I had cut the stripes off a tunic belonging to one of us who had not received a commission. His ire was somewhat assuaged by my paying for having them sewn on again.

Those of us who were commissioned were given a clothing allowance of $100 to help with our purchases of officers' uniforms. This money covered only the basic necessities, such as one uniform, cap, and greatcoat. The presence of the SFTS must have been a bonanza for Saskatoon's tailors as with each graduating course there was a number of newly-commissioned officers who needed to be outfitted. It can be said that the tailors provided fast service, most uniforms being ready in 24 hours. It was with more than a considerable degree of self-conscious pride that I stepped out into the street complete with black oxfords, brown leather gloves and pilot's wings shining on my left breast—a "flat hat in flying cloth."

We were granted two weeks' leave before reporting to our next posting, in my case to 31 General Reconnaissance School (RAF) at Charlottetown, P.E.I. As GRS was considered the basic training for Coastal Command it seemed my dream of becoming a fighter pilot was just that—a dream from which I was about to be wakened.

CHAPTER 6

General Reconnaissance School

General Reconnaissance School was a new experience for us in several ways. First, it was our initiation into the rites and formalities of an RAF officers' mess. Secondly, we were informed immediately that all of our flying would be as navigators, again on the much despised Avro Anson Mk I. Thirdly, some of our time and instruction would deal with naval matters as GRS was the preparatory course for Coastal Command in which we would be required to work in cooperation with allied naval vessels or perhaps, against German, Italian or Japanese naval units.

The duration of the course was approximately eight weeks during which I logged 43 hours and 45 minutes on fourteen flights. Far more time was spent in ground school delving into the intricacies of various navigation techniques used for flying over the sea. We also learned to do creeping-line-ahead and square searches, astro-navigation, reconnaissance techniques, compasses and compass swinging, meteorology, wireless and visual signals and coding, ship recognition, and photography.

Fortunately the weather was pleasant most of the time so it was no hardship to spend many hours in the evenings on the lawn of the quarters taking innumerable star shots with a sextant in order to familiarize ourselves with its use and to establish our "average error" to be applied to our astral observations in the future.

Ship recognition was strongly emphasized and we soon became adept at identifying various classes of warships of the combatant nations. Here we amused ourselves by relating the features of various classes of ships to their national origins. German warships, for example, looked neat and efficient in design with little clutter whereas Japanese battle wagons had their masts loaded with so much gear they looked like pagodas. The Italian character, we joked, was evident in the fact that many of their capital ships had the bulk of their main armament aft—a single heavy gun turret forward, with two at the stern—thereby indicating they preferred to bring their maximum firepower to bear while leaving a battle rather than going into one.

Flying over Prince Edward Island in late spring and early summer was a visual delight. The contrast between green fields, rolling green-clad hills and the orange-red soil was remarkably pretty. On calm sunny days the shading of colours in the water where red beaches slid under the blue-green sea was unlike anything we had ever seen or would ever see again. These same beaches became havens of relaxation for us on our occasional days off, swimming and sunning ourselves in relative solitude.

It was remarkable to us that we seldom encountered local people on the beaches we frequented. On one occasion, however, I did meet one of the locals. I was swimming with a crawl stroke in no particular direction when I bumped into something round, soft and definitely feminine. I apologized while treading water, and we swam together to where we could stand on the bottom. Here we exchanged names and proceeded to the beach where, as the water shoaled, like Aphrodite emerging from the sea and just as lovely, she was revealed in a skin-tight white bathing suit. She spent the rest of the afternoon with me and two of my air force friends and her personality seemed as pleasing as her appearance. She was a native of Charlottetown who was home from attending university on the mainland. Regrettably, I never saw her again.

Charlottetown offered little in the way of social diversion beyond movies and a few restaurants. At that time the island was completely dry, even beyond the exigencies of wartime liquor rationing. The only way to obtain liquor was with a doctor's prescription to which we, as air force personnel with our own medical services, had no access.

Occasionally there was a public dance held in the town and my friends and I attended one. Here I met a pretty young woman who, it seemed, offered the "open sesame" to all sorts of goodies. She had a car belonging to her father who, she explained, through some political boondoggles had an unlimited gasoline ration and as many doctor's prescriptions for booze as one could wish. It seemed too good to be true. It was.

We left the dance and drove into the country where we parked in a secluded spot. Almost immediately she threw herself at me in a very sexual way and it was obvious it was her intention to have sex as quickly as possible. I still felt my allegiance was to my girlfriend in Saskatoon and was further deterred by the obvious risk of relations with someone so evidently promiscuous. I fended her off, drove the car to the gate of the RAF station, thanked her for the ride, and left. I never saw her again either, but this time there were no regrets.

Meanwhile, our training progressed. Our navigation instructor was a pleasant RAF navigator, Flying Officer Monger. He, we learned, had joined the RAF early in the war and had gone on operations in Handley Page Hampdens, an aircraft that was obsolete before the war began. We learned also that of the course of navigators with whom he had trained, he at that time was the sole survivor. I sincerely hope he lasted out the war.

The commanding officer of the station was a rather antique RAF Group Captain (G/C) who was somewhat eccentric, to put it mildly. Our first encounter with his rules was in the matter of flying suits. We had been equipped with the heavy canvas RAF variety on arrival at the station and were informed that they were to be worn at all times in the air. The CO believed they offered protection against fire. We had heard many derogatory reports about the Anson, and had had some experience with it ourselves, but never had we heard it was any more of a fire risk than any other aircraft of its day. Flying at low altitudes over the sea in sunny summer weather in the "Flying Greenhouse" was not a cooling experience.

Before a flight, burdened with large canvas nav bags, sextants, bulky and heavy cameras, we made our way across the hot asphalt tarmac, sweat literally coursing down our bodies under our uniforms and the heavy flying suits, and mounted the aircraft. As soon as we were airborne the stripping began and the flying suits were tossed into the rear of the aircraft until we landed again. We were not alone in this action—staff pilots and navigation instructors also defied the CO's dictum.

My only direct personal encounter with the Group Captain happened one sunny morning after a rainstorm had swept the station during the night. A friend and I were making our way to the Mess for breakfast when we encountered the CO who was bound for the same destination. Customarily he arrived at the station from his residence in Charlottetown by staff car which he abandoned at the gate and walked to the mess. After exchanging salutes and "Good Mornings," we proceeded along the road with him until we came to the sidewalk leading from the roadway to the front door of the Mess. It was covered from side to side by a large puddle of rainwater through which we would have to wade. The CO stopped, eyed the puddle with an outraged expression and snapped at us, "Who put that water there? Who put that water there? Have them take it away! Have them take it away!"

After a baleful look in our direction he tiptoed through the puddle and entered the Mess. We did the same after unsuccessfully trying to suppress our laughter.

Once a week a CO's parade was held on the parade square, first thing in the morning. On one occasion the parade was formed up ready for CO's inspection, but no CO. We were stood "at ease" awaiting his arrival which came about after only a few minutes. Ignoring all of the usual protocol associated with taking over the parade, he marched straight to the reviewing stand and made an announcement which went something like this: "I called this parade for Oh-eight hundred hours. It is now O-eight-O-seven. I am seven minutes late. I am confining myself to the station for seven days. Parade, dismiss!" The parade dissolved in confusion and, as far as we knew, he didn't go home for seven days.

A friend of mine who got married after getting his wings brought his bride with him to Charlottetown. He applied for an SOP—a "Sleeping Out Pass." As he later related the story to us he was paraded before the CO who, after making a derisive comment about bloody colonials having to take their wives everywhere with them and lecturing him on the need for perfect attendance and punctuality, granted the pass. Apparently he thought nothing of the incongruity of his remarks when he had brought his own wife from the U.K. by sea in hazardous wartime conditions.

There was another incident, which I did not witness personally but have no reason to doubt, because it was told to us by one of the RAF instructors on the station. It involved the air test of an Anson after overhaul. The CO announced that he would do the test and arrived on the scene in a non-regulation white flying suit. He started the aircraft up, taxied it to the end of the runway in use, ran up the engines, then shut them down and walked back to the hangars where he announced that the aircraft was serviceable! We speculated that the RAF had posted him to "the colonies" to get him out of their hair while he served out his time to retirement.

Most of our flying time was occupied stoogeing around the Gulf of St. Lawrence performing various navigation exercises with little to break the monotony. We learned to take drifts with dropped smoke floats, to read wind lanes on the surface of the sea and to navigate an aircraft to approximately where we were supposed to go. However, there were a few exciting moments, one of which was definitely not included in the course.

We were flying with an RAF sergeant staff pilot who was obviously very cheesed off with his boring duty. Our flight took us to the Gaspé Peninsula within sight of the huge pierced rock off Percé. A natural arch had been formed by wave action through a giant, vertically-sided, long and narrow rock off shore which, viewed end on, looked like a great ship ploughing through the waves. From the side, the arch could be seen near the seaward end of the 70-or 80-foot-high formation. Our pilot announced to us that he was going to fly through the arch. We objected violently that the arch was not wide enough for an Anson to pass through. It was only after a few minutes of heated argument that we were able to dissuade him from the attempt. I believe, fifty years later, that the configuration of the rock has been changed by further erosion but I am positive that in 1943 the arch was not wide enough. I have wondered, too, if the pilot might have been pulling our legs and had no real intention of trying to fly through it. If so, I wonder how many students he put through the same terrifying ordeal.

Another day we arrived for our pre-flight briefing to find things in a state of excitement. Apparently a U-boat had been reported in the Gulf and we were to search for it in the vicinity of the Magdalen Islands (Iles de la Madeleine). Needless to say, we were just as excited as everyone else and took off for the search amid dreams of glory. We didn't find it. From the perspective of later experience, I can only thank God we didn't. A plodding Anson, which could barely get airborne carrying a full crew, one depth charge and one fixed forward-firing .30-calibre machine gun, would have had about as much chance against a determined U-boat crew as the proverbial snowball in the hot place.

One of our training exercises was to do a photographic reconnaissance of one of the small harbours toward the east end of the island. This was accomplished by having the pilot position the aircraft in such a manner that a student with a hand-held camera could photograph whatever shipping happened to be in the harbour. This was done by holding the bulky and heavy camera, which was about 14 inches square and the same length, partly out the window in the door of the aircraft.

When my turn came to do such a recce all went well up to and during the picture taking. Then, as we approached the end of the run, the pilot pulled the aircraft up sharply into a steep climbing turn. I was still holding the camera part way out the window when it suddenly doubled or tripled in weight as the G-force of the pull-up took hold. By the time its weight returned to normal it was all the way outside of the aircraft being buffeted by the slipstream with me hanging on to it for dear life. Fortunately, I was able to hold on but if the added G had lasted a second or two longer, the RAF would have been short one very expensive camera and I, in all probability, would have had at least a good part of its value deducted from my pay.

A routine deduction from our pay was our bar bills. Each officer had a bar book into which was entered the value of every drink he purchased at the bar, the sum of which was added to his mess bill at the end of the month. Students were limited to a certain maximum amount each month. Exceeding the limit brought what was known in the RAF as "tea and cakes with the CO." This could be avoided, of course, by using someone else's bar book and paying its owner cash for the drinks put on it but this subterfuge seldom was necessary.

Another thing to which we were introduced in the Mess bar was overproof rum. This liquor proved almost disastrous for my roommate in the quarters. He had come down with a severe cold and decided the overproof rum was the treatment he needed. He proceeded to consume several doubles in rapid succession while sitting in a comfortable easy chair close to a good fire in the fireplace. A short time later we noticed he was sound asleep. Our efforts to waken him were unavailing so three of us carried him back to the quarters and dumped him on his bed. He scarcely stirred until the next morning when he awoke with a severe hangover—and an even worse cold!

I managed, quite unintentionally, to put up a major "black" in the mess. When I received my wings after SFTS my parents had given me a beautiful and very expensive wristwatch made by Tissot. One day when alone in the quarters I forgetfully left the watch on the shelf above the wash basins which were in the cross bar of the H-shaped barrack block. It was only a matter of a few minutes before I went to retrieve it. There had been no one else in the washroom with me and there was still no one visible when I returned—but my watch was gone. There were two possibilities facing me. Either my watch had been stolen or, hopefully, another officer had retrieved it for safe-keeping and would return it to me. In hope the latter was the case, I drafted a notice and put it on the bulletin board in the mess, unaware that in an RAF mess it was necessary to get the President of the Mess Committee's permission to post a notice.

Before dinner that evening I was hauled up on the carpet before the Squadron Leader PMC and given a double dressing down: first, for posting the notice without permission and, secondly, as he read it, for accusing some officer of being a thief. My rejoinder that if the watch was not returned then someone was a thief, was not well received. Any further action by me, such as notifying the service police, was forbidden. I left the office somewhat the wiser about mess protocol but high-ly irate. I never saw the watch again.

My own belief was and is that it was not taken by another officer. At the time the RAF quarters were staffed by batmen brought over from Britain. They were known as General Duties personnel, the lowest of the low in the RAF trade structure and their pay, in Canadian terms, was a pittance. At the time my watch was taken a draft of these men had already been named for return to Britain and they departed the station only a day or two later. I strongly suspect that my watch pre-ceded me overseas with one of them. I purchased another watch from a shop in Charlottetown, a Rolex as close in appearance to the original as I could find, but not nearly as valuable. I could never bring myself to tell my parents about the loss of their gift but its substitute served me faithfully until long after the war.

The mess provided diversions in the form of billiards and darts. This was our fist encounter with the English dartboard which was practical-ly unknown in Canada before the war. We took up the game enthusi-astically but seldom achieved anything like the skill at it displayed by some of our British mess members who could consistently throw darts into the "double top" to get their game under way.

But the most amusing incident in the Mess during our stay there took place in the dining room one day late in July. The kitchen served corn-on-the-cob for dinner. It was obviously a puzzle to our British companions and we watched in amused amazement as they began to tackle it with knife and fork. There was a great variety of techniques employed from trying to pry the corn off one kernel at a time with a fork to trying to slice it off with a knife while attempting, usually unsuccessfully, to hold the cob securely with a fork. We began to eat it in the Canadian manner, smearing it liberally with butter and holding the cobs in our fingers. Many RAF personnel eyed this procedure with obvious contempt but others soon followed suit. Some gave up in disgust and with comments like, "Cattle feed!" declined to eat it at all. However, those who took the lead from us obviously enjoyed what to them was a very novel food.

Not long before the course ended we were all summoned to a room where we were sat on the floor, one at a time, with our backs firmly against a wall and our legs extended straight out while an NCO measured our seated leg length. We were told the purpose of this was to determine who among us could fly Liberators which, it was stated, required pilots to have long legs to cope with its rudder pedals under emergency conditions. When one considers the hundreds of British, Canadian and American pilots who flew Libs during the war, one wonders if they all had extra long legs!

The course ended with all of us obtaining RAF Navigators' Certificates, Second Class, and our next postings. For most of us it was to "Y" Depot in Halifax—in other words, overseas. Two or three were posted to the Bahamas to go on Coastal Command Liberators but I, for one, was happy with the overseas posting. It seemed to offer at least a possibility of fulfilling my dream of becoming a fighter pilot although my having qualified as a GR pilot for Coastal Command was not a good omen for the future. I certainly didn't look forward to spending the rest of the war flying over the North Atlantic.

CHAPTER 7

Halifax, New York, New York, Montreal, Halifax

On leaving GRS we were granted embarkation leave. I returned to Saskatoon and to my home town by train, at that time the only available means of long-distance transportation. Happily, as commissioned officers, we were given transportation warrants to cover our fare plus sleeping car berths which gave us access to the club car, although Canadian trains then were "dry." There seemed to be a chumminess among club car passengers which made such a trip a pleasant experience. It put us in touch with many people from various strata of society with whom, in other circumstances, we might not have had contact.

On arrival in Saskatoon I made a decision which I have regretted ever since. As the future for me was heavily clouded and there was a distinct possibility that I might not return from overseas, I decided that both for her sake and mine, it would be better if I broke off with my girlfriend. My intentions were both altruistic and selfish because I felt I had no right to insist that she should remain true to me, and I also felt that I, too, should be free. I know that my action caused her pain for which I am still sorry. Happily, three years later I was able to repair the breech and we married.

From Saskatoon I proceeded to my home town of Dinsmore where I found an old friend, also in the air force, home on leave and another friend who had been found unfit for military service. We were the only males there of the group I had grown up with. Of all the other young men of our age most were in the services while a few had taken jobs in distant places, some in wartime industries. One particularly good friend of mine was in Fort William working in a factory building Hawker Hurricane fighter planes.

The break-up of my relationship with my girlfriend led to what began as a delightful, but ended as a terrifying, experience. I made the acquaintance of a pretty young woman from Ontario of about my own age who was visiting a local family. We went to the movies together. One evening we were engaged in some rather passionate petting in a car parked in front of the home in which she was visiting. Suddenly I felt her body go limp and she stopped breathing. For a moment I was stunned.

Not knowing quite what I could do in the cramped front seat of the car, I tried a simulation of artificial respiration by wrapping my arms around her chest and squeezing sharply in an approximation of a rapid breathing rhythm. Mouth to mouth resuscitation was unknown at that time but I think I became one of its earliest successful practitioners as I clamped my mouth over hers and blew in an alternating rhythm with my squeezing of her chest. After what was probably only two or three minutes but which seemed like hours her eyes fluttered open and she began breathing again. She seemed to be unaware that anything unusual had happened and when I told her what a fright she had given me she was astonished. After a minute or two I escorted her carefully to the front door of the house and bade her goodnight. Upon returning to the car I noticed that it was my breathing now which was laboured and erratic. It was an experience which I did not care to repeat—and didn't.

At the end of my leave came the farewells to my mother and father. As they already had lost one son in the war, I was sure it would be much harder for them than for me. But my mother astonished me by declaring she was sure I would return safely. She said that when my brother went to England in the RAF in the dark days just before the war began she had felt she would never see him again but that in my case she felt just as sure I would survive. It was an expression of faith which I held always close to my heart

The return trip to Halifax turned into a reunion as service friends boarded the train at nearly every stop. During the lay-over in Montreal between trains, two officer friends from Winnipeg and I were strolling the streets enjoying the sights when we were approached by a dapper man who asked us if we would like to see a "French circus" featuring pretty girls. We accepted and were escorted to a house to the east of the downtown area. We were led into a room which contained a few chairs and a large low circular bed.

After paying our admission fee of five dollars each, we were given a drink of rye and seated. Three women who appeared to be in their mid-twenties entered, stark naked, and gave the performance constituting the "circus." This consisted of them twining their bodies around one another lasciviously on the round bed with much caressing of breasts, fingering of pubic areas and performance of cunnilingus on one another. When the performance ended we were invited to enjoy the other delights of the place. We declined and we were soon on our way back downtown, somewhat shaken by the whole experience. Certainly none of us had ever seen such a wanton display of female flesh. The strange thing to me is that all I can recall of their appearance is an appendectomy scar on one woman's belly.

We repaired to the cocktail lounge of the Mount Royal Hotel where we again encountered three or four friends who were en route to Halifax. Here we hatched a plan to survive the monotony of the trip.

It was agreed that three of us would exchange our berths on the train for an "A" drawing room which would be HQ for the group. To provide some liquid pleasure we found it simple, with a lounge waiter as intermediary, to arrange for the purchase of a bottle of scotch, the actual transaction taking place on the front steps of the hotel. So much for the effectiveness of wartime liquor rationing in Montreal! In fact, the greatest deterrent to the unbridled use of such a source was the price of bootlegged liquor which, at $30 a bottle, in those days was astronomical.

The first stop for the train after leaving Montreal was in Lévis, across the St. Lawrence River from Quebec City. Our very cooperative porter informed us that beer was available in a grocery store just across a street from where our sleeping car was stopped. Accordingly, as he indicated we would have plenty of time, we ran across the street in a group and proceeded to buy a supply of beer. On being informed that an individual could purchase only three "quart" bottles at a time, we appointed one of our number to stand guard outside while the rest of us bought our ration, raced outside, deposited it on the sidewalk, and returned to the end of the line to purchase more. We went back to the train with every available pocket filled and bottles of beer stacked like kindling on our arms. When it was all placed on the floor of the drawing room, the only way one could walk across the floor was by carefully placing one's feet on the caps of the upright bottles.

Although it may sound rather extreme, our party had grown so large by this time that there was barely seating space for all of us on the two facing seats and the one running fore and aft along the interior wall. In fact, our liquor supply ran out long before we reached Halifax but we were able to supplement it with a bottle of bourbon supplied by the porter—for a price.

Suddenly the lights went out in our drawing room. We waited. Nothing happened. Someone opened the door. All was darkness. He struck a match. The train was empty! Our friendly porter had neglected to notify us we had arrived in Halifax. The train had been moved clear of the station and shut down, thus extinguishing the lights. After collecting our hand luggage we made our way along the tracks for what seemed about half a mile to the station. Fortunately, our heavy luggage had all been checked. We were bussed to the "Y" Depot, allotted quarters, and began the long wait for the journey overseas.

Our time at "Y" Depot was pretty much our own except for a daily roll call. We spent hours roaming the streets of Halifax and, on the advice of those who had been through it all before, purchasing items which we were told were hard to come by in Britain such as cigarette lighters. Some invested in silk stockings and fine lingerie as potential items of barter. It was while purchasing a cigarette lighter at the jewellery counter in Eatons that I met a pretty young woman whom I was able to persuade to go out on a date with me. Better, she also arranged partners for a couple of my friends, and we formed a congenial group which endured for the duration of our stay.

Although we didn't drink a great deal, it was nice on occasion to have a drink together. This was made possible by the fact that the uncle of one of the girls in our group was employed in the liquor store. After being introduced to him we purchased the occasional bottle at his wicket where he would ostensibly stamp our liquor ration books but managed to miss the book each time. When we finally left Halifax my Nova Scotia ration book was as pristine as the day I had purchased it.

Our stay in "Y" Depot in Halifax was largely a matter of killing time while we waited for a ship to take us across the Atlantic. We were kitted up with steel helmets, respirators and web equipment. The latter was issued to us in assorted bits and pieces which we took back to our quarters and put together. It was rather like doing a flexible jig-saw puzzle. The webbing consisted of a three-inch wide adjustable blue belt with brass fittings, a heavy canvas pouch to hang from the belt, a pistol holster and two shoulder straps which, when the outfit was assembled properly, crossed in the back and supported all the rest.

I learned quickly that a steel helmet didn't protect one against all types of blows. Two or three of us were attempting to assemble the web equipment, I sitting on the floor with the various bits scattered around me. A friend entered the room behind me and walloped me on top of the head with a heavy broom. As the head band in the steel helmet had not yet been properly adjusted the force of the blow exerted itself directly on my skull on which the helmet was resting—and practically drove my head down between my shoulders. I was incapacitated for a couple of minutes and I believe that was closest I had ever come to being knocked out. Needless to say, there were some harsh words exchanged.

A bright sunny day persuaded a friend and me to go boating and our expedition almost ended in disaster. We rented a canoe from one of the boat clubs on the Northwest Arm and set out to enjoy the sunshine. We paddled toward the mouth of the Arm and nearing it, saw there was an aircraft carrier and a group of escort vessels anchored not far off. We decided to pay the carrier a visit and began paddling toward it. What we hadn't counted on was the difference in wave activity between the sheltered Arm and the more open water outside. As we progressed beyond the mouth of the Arm the waves kept increasing in size until soon we were paddling up and down four-or five-foot watery slopes with not much more than a canoe's length between them. It took little of this to convince us that any attempt to reach the carrier could be the last mistake we would ever make so we decided to return. But how could we get the canoe turned around? Happily, the waves were running almost at right angles to our course so up to this point there had been little danger of tipping but the thought of turning the canoe broadside to them was more than a little worrisome. Up to this point I had been paddling in the stern of the canoe so I held it headed into the waves while my companion made an about face on his seat. Then he performed the same service for me and we returned with me paddling in what was now the bow. I think we both heaved great sighs of relief on reaching the relatively calm waters inside the Arm.

One day early in September a hundred pilots were called out and informed we were going to New York to board a ship. It was then that we had what was euphemistically called an "overseas medical." This turned out to be what was known in the service as a "short arms inspection." We were lined up in a drill hall and told to open our flies and take out our penises. A medical officer then walked up and down the line eyeing our private parts and instructing each of us in turn to "milk it." We assumed the object of the exercise was to see if any of us were infected with VD. As no one was fallen out of the draft, I guess we were all considered medically fit for overseas service.

We travelled by train to New York and were immediately marched aboard a ship, the *Scythia*, a passenger liner. As officers we were allotted cabins on the upper decks. All of the furniture had been removed from the cabins and replaced with triple-tiered-bunks so up to a dozen of us were crammed into what had been a cabin for a single passenger or a couple in peace time. In addition to our group of Canadians, there were on the upper decks a large number of white American Army officers and a group of white American Army nurses. In the lower decks every available space had been equipped with three and four levels of bunks and was filled with black American soldiers and their gear. Sardines in a can have almost as much space!

During our first day at sea we were impressed by the magnitude of the operation of which we now were a part. There were six former passenger liners formed up in two lines ahead of three ships each. In the middle, between the two lines of passenger ships was a warship which, from our ship recognition classes, we were able to identify as a Nevada class battleship. Ahead of this array, almost out of sight, was a line of cruisers and, we were told, ahead of them but out of our range of vision a line of destroyers.

The weather was beautiful but as we set out on the open sea we encountered a long, huge swell running almost directly across our course. The battleship seemed to ignore the swell and ploughed through it with a minimum of up and down motion but the passenger ships were constantly pitching fore and aft with the bows rising fifteen or twenty feet and then plunging downward into the trough between the swells. We learned it was something of a trick to walk down stairs when the next step one expected to reach had suddenly dropped several feet.

Some of us were assigned to duty watch. Our task was to patrol certain areas below decks during the night, mostly to ensure that no one was smoking. With all of the gear in such close quarters plus several thousand kapok-filled life jackets, a fire would have been catastrophic. But the pitching of the ship in the swell had had a disastrous effect on the closely-confined troops below decks. We joked that if there were 5000 troops on board, 4,999 of them were seasick.

My patrol area was on a lower deck forward on the port side, so far forward that one "wall" was formed by the angled shear of the bow making the space almost triangular. Its position so far forward ensured it was getting the full benefit of the rise and fall of the bow in the swell. On my first inspection of the area I stepped over the coaming at the door and almost landed on my rump as my feet slipped in a considerable depth of human vomit oozing back and forth on the deck. The stench was overpowering. I backed out and commented to the senior NCO who was my companion on duty that I was sure no one was going to smoke in there that night. I didn't set foot in the area again. That was the closest I ever came to being seasick myself. Fortunately, because of the number of officers available, we were given such duty for one night only.

After two days at sea we were informed by the ship's loudspeaker system that the ship was experiencing boiler problems and was going to return to New York. A destroyer was detached from the convoy's escort to accompany us. Our ship turned around but was still cutting across the swell almost at right angles. We re-entered New York Harbor early in the evening of our fourth day since setting sail. By this time we had been in calm waters for a considerable period of time so many of the seasick soldiers had recovered and several hundred of them crowded onto the forward well deck. Many of we officers lined the rails of an upper deck just two or three feet above their heads. As we passed by the Statue of Liberty one of the blacks called out quite emphatically, "Lady, if you gonna see me again, you gonna hafta turn around!" And there is a sequel to this story. Several years later I saw it retold in an American magazine's military humour section and can only assume it was sent in by one of the many American Army officers standing beside me that day.

The next morning the loudspeaker system instructed all Royal Canadian Air Force personnel to report to a particular deck area, where we were informed we were being taken off the ship. First, we were conducted to a baggage hold and instructed to pick out our luggage. Each of us was equipped with two light blue half-trunks, standard equipment for RCAF officers at the time, with our names and regimental numbers painted on the outside. As these were all in one area of the hold and were completely unlike American Army luggage, the task was relatively simple. Our luggage identified, we were told it would be unloaded from the ship and would follow us. A short time later we marched down a gangplank off of the ship to the accompaniment of a barrage of catcalls from the thousands of Americans we were leaving behind on the reeking vessel.

We were bussed to Grand Central Station where we were lined up and told there was a train leaving at 1 a.m. for Montreal. We were ordered tersely, "Be on it!" and were dismissed. As it was still just shortly after noon, we all looked forward to a day and evening in New York. We descended on the check room en masse and encountered our first problem: the check room staff absolutely refused to take charge of 100 sets of identical web equipment, 100 respirators and 100 steel helmets. We were all unhappily faced with the prospect of carting this gear all over New York with us. Then one of our number walked out into the middle of the concourse, removed his unwanted gear, looped the straps together and dropped it on the floor. "That'll be there when I come back," he declared. We all followed suit and in moments there was a great pile of webbing, respirators and steel helmets awaiting our return.

Three or four of us who had never been in New York decided we would walk up 42nd Street to Broadway, stopping for one drink in every bar we passed—a plan which we soon had to abandon as there were too many drinking spots on our route. We finally reached Broadway and proceeded along it, enjoying the sights, eventually arriving back at the Astor Hotel on Times Square. Here we had dinner and spent most of the evening in the Astor Roof nightclub listening to the dance music of Tommy Tucker's band. Unfortunately, there were practically no unattached females so we didn't dance.

All too soon it was time for us to make our exit to catch our train, so the hotel doorman called up a taxi for us. The driver had evidently encountered a few other Canadian service personnel because as we piled into the cab, he commented, "I know. Grand Central station." Others of our group were arriving at the same time and we all headed for the pile of gear we had left. It was still there but as time for boarding the train was fast approaching, most of us made little effort to find our own webbing. We hastily grabbed a set and headed for the train. On board we found the berths all made up so sorting out the gear seemed like an almost impossible task. We all wished to find our own as we had our personal toiletries in the pouch of the webbing. I walked through the coach in which my berth was located and near the far end saw a pair of RCAF-trousered legs and shoes sticking out through the curtains. I pulled back the curtain and showed him the webbing I had. Unbelievably, it was his—and he had mine! Figure the odds!

Many of us made our way to the club car where we found what seemed to be a big party in full swing. On seeing our uniforms a portly gentleman, who we later learned was a Puerto Rican sugar entrepreneur, waved us over to his table and insisted on buying us drinks. In broken English he congratulated us on our success in the Battle of Britain. The fact that the famous battle took place two years before we were even in the Air Force and that our shoulder badges clearly indicated we were Canadian, not British, were of little moment to him and he continued to purchase drinks until the bar closed when the train reached the Canadian border.

On arrival in Montreal a few of us hailed a taxi and had it take us to the nearest YMCA. Here we luxuriated in hot showers and spent some time in the swimming pool. We felt considerably better in spite of the fact we had to put on the same clothing we had worn since we left Halifax almost a week before. We didn't know it but it would be a long time yet before we encountered our luggage again—on the other side of the Atlantic! We later described ourselves as the "highest" pilots ever to reach England.

We were in Halifax for only a day or two before we were paraded to the dock behind the Nova Scotian Hotel and onto the liner *Queen Elizabeth*. About a dozen of us were allotted bunks in what had been, in happier times, the dressing room of a first-class suite. Although the quarters were cramped we had one advantage—the suite's bathroom was available to us, including a tub and shower. We soon learned the water supplied for bathing was sea water in which our ordinary toilet soap was practically useless. Also, the water was turned on for only a relatively short period each day so it was not unusual for one of us to be caught only half-rinsed or not rinsed at all when the water suddenly ceased to flow.

The food was excellent, at least in the officers' dining room although we heard tales that the situation was far different on the lower decks where the other ranks were quartered. Each of us was assigned to a "sitting" and table for the voyage and we were served two meals a day, breakfast and dinner. The times were determined by the sitting. Thus, assigned to the first sitting, our group ate breakfast at 0730 and dined at 1730.

The QE sailed without escort, relying on her speed to make her a very elusive target for enemy U-boats. However, she was armed with a large deck gun aft, manned by naval personnel and several machine gun positions to which some of the air gunners on board were assigned. Fortunately, on our voyage none of these had to be used. The only incident which might have been due to some indication of enemy action was a very sharp turn to port at one point.

At the time I was seated in one of the lounges and, along with much of the furniture and its occupants. I slid halfway across the lounge as the ship heeled steeply to starboard. The only thing that remained immobile during this manoeuvre was one of the stewards who, a tray balanced on one hand with practised ease remained firmly rooted to the spot where he was standing, albeit with his body at what appeared to be about a 30-degree angle to the deck.

The weather was beautiful for the entire crossing. The ocean was quite calm so the ship was very steady, in sharp contrast to our experience aboard the *Scythia* a few days before. On the fourth day after leaving Halifax we sailed past the rocky shores of western Scotland and on the fifth, up the Firth of Clyde to Greenock where the ship anchored.

We disembarked on 19 September, the sixth day after our having boarded the ship in Halifax. We were immediately put on a train which was to take us the length of England to Bournemouth on the south coast. This was the location of the RCAF's No.3 Personnel Reception Centre. The overnight trip was a memorable one from the point of view of discomfort with four of us assigned to two facing seats in a coach. We were served our first English meal in the coach and the food did not augur well for the future—a plate of an unappetizing mutton stew and a slice of greyish wartime bread. So it was "Welcome to wartime Britain!"

CHAPTER 8

No. 3 Personnel Reception Centre

We arrived at No. 3 PRC in Bournemouth, Hants. (How did the English abbreviate "Hampshire" to "Hants?"), in the morning. We were in a very bedraggled state, unshaven and bleary-eyed after an uncomfortable night on the train, during which three of us shared two double seats while a fourth stretched out on the floor. Needless to say, we had slept very little.

For breakfast we were taken to the Officers' Mess, located in one of the big waterfront hotels, and then to quarters allotted to us in the Highcliffe Hotel. This was the first of three hotels in which we were to live during the six weeks we were in Bournemouth but the reason for us being shunted from one hotel to another was never revealed to us. I presume the PRC was located in Bournemouth because of its many hotels. Bournemouth was a pre-war resort town and the war put an end to the tourist business.

Our accommodation was far from luxurious. We were four to a room containing four standard RAF beds and a washbasin with taps which most often stubbornly refused to emit any hot water. There were no chests of drawers so we were constantly burrowing in our 12-by-30-by-16-inch half-trunks in hopes of finding a pair of clean socks or a shirt which didn't look like it had spent its youth in an accordion. The arrival of our half-trunks was a major relief because we had not had them since departing Halifax to go to New York more than two weeks before. Consequently we had been attired only in the clothes we wore, with wrinkled hand-washed shirts and underclothing still carrying salt from being washed aboard ship—seawater being all that was available in our quarters.

Most of our days in Bournemouth were spent killing time. The air force laid on occasional duties in an attempt to keep us occupied but most were of a hit and miss variety. Once we were taken out for physical training and were given a strenuous workout which nearly laid us all low as we had had very little physical activity for many weeks. It happened only once while we were there so its value was very dubious. Again, we spent a week on a naval familiarization course conducted by Royal Navy personnel who gave us the definite impression they thought they were wasting their time—which they were. The course left no lasting impression with me at all.

Once we were paraded to a movie theatre where we were shown some real horror movies, about VD. That did leave an impression! Nothing of the consequences of VD was left to the imagination. However, some of the effect was lost when the last film was shown. It had been made for the U.S. Army in Hollywood and the young actress who played the role of the disease carrier was stunningly beautiful. The theatre was filled with whistles of approval and loudly voiced comments such as, "Wow! I'd take a chance on her any day!"

Most of our days were spent walking around the town familiarizing ourselves with things British. We remarked with surprise on the displays of chocolate in some shop windows but soon learned it was strictly rationed and we had no ration coupons. But there seemed to be an inexhaustible supply of tea in the many tearooms in the town and we made it a habit to stop in at one or another of them nearly every afternoon. In one, we were surprised to see hamburgers on the menu. A friend ordered one but the rest of us demurred. The waitress brought him some sort of a pastry bun with a bit of grilled meat about the size o a quarter hidden in it. As she put it down she leaned over for a closer look and remarked, "I've never seen a hamburger before." Our friend opened the bun, peered at it and replied, "Lady, you haven't seen one yet."

One day a friend and I rented bicycles and set out to tour the town. The bikes were in terrible shape. Mine had no brakes on the rear wheel and very little effective braking on the front. At one point in our tour we were faced with descending a long steep hill. We were only a short way down when the little braking capability of my bike gave out completely and bike and I accelerated at a truly alarming rate. At the bottom of the hill the street was a dead end and I faced a stone wall which seemed to be approaching at very high speed.

I still don't know how I managed it but I made a turn at the bottom by jumping the "kerb" and zipping between a soldier standing with his girlfriend at a bus stop and the stone wall, on a sidewalk about four feet wide! I am sure I was going at least 30 miles an hour. Shortly thereafter my friend's bike developed a flat tire and we concluded the tour by pushing the bikes miles back to the shop where we had rented them.

Of course, we were confounded by the traffic rules and frequently found ourselves unwittingly riding on the wrong side of the street. Fortunately for us, there was so little traffic in a town like Bournemouth during the war that we escaped calamity. But it did take us a time to learn to look first to the right instead of the left when stepping onto a street.

The highlight of our time at Bournemouth was a week's debarkation leave. I was invited by a friend to accompany him to the home of his English aunt who lived in Sevenoaks, Kent. After picking up leave passes, transportation warrants and ration books (subsequently turned over to our hostess so she could feed us) we took a train to London. We had enough time to wander around the Mother of Parliaments and have lunch in a restaurant before taking a taxi to Waterloo Junction. There we boarded what we now would call a commuter train to Sevenoaks. And we had to learn quickly that one didn't hesitate when boarding these trains. It seemed to us it only stopped for about thirty seconds before pulling out again.

We telephoned the aunt when we arrived in Sevenoaks and she explained how to get to her home. We walked and found it without difficulty although this was our first exposure to the English custom of naming houses rather than giving them street numbers. The house we sought was named Kennet and was located on a street called The Drive. We were received by our hostess and her husband with great friendliness and were quickly made to feel right at home. We spent the better part of a week with them and found it very relaxing-pleasant company, good food, good reading material and enjoyable walks exploring the area. During the six days we were there I managed to get through a large portion of Samuel Pepys Diary.

We were particularly fascinated by a large estate with an immense house called Knole House which had been built at the time of Queen Elizabeth I. She gave it to the family that still resided in it. We were told it had 365 rooms. We were also astounded by the deer in the surrounding park. They were beautifully proportioned animals, some with full racks of antlers but, to us, tiny! They were about the size of, or even smaller than, our pronghorn antelope.

The second day there we decided to go walking in civilian clothes we had brought with us. We had hardly got nicely into our walk when we were stopped by a bobby who demanded identification. Young men of military age in civilian clothes were a rarity in England. After showing him our ID cards, he became quite friendly and told us they had heard there were a couple of escaped German POWs somewhere in the area and it was quite likely we would be stopped by every policeman we met. We didn't meet another but that night we put our "civvies" away. I never wore mine again all the time I was in the UK.

Another reminder of the war we encountered on that leave was truck loads of Italian POWs being taken out to work on farms in the area. It was a sight to which we were to become quite accustomed in other parts of Britain as well. In the evenings we were fascinated by our host's description of the Blitz, and of the Battle of Britain, much of which took place practically over their heads. One morning we were informed by our hosts that there had been an air raid alarm during the night. Neither my friend nor I had heard a thing but slept soundly through our first air raid. However, it had turned out to be a false alarm.

While at Sevenoaks we bussed to Westerham, our first ride on an English double-decker bus. Here we saw General Wolfe's statue and home. Wolfe is of particular interest to me because there is a tradition in our family that we are in some way related to him although I have never been able to find out just how. We also looked into the "George and Dragon" pub, where Wolfe is reputed to have had his last meal in Westerham before leaving for Canada and his death.

From Westerham we bussed again to Biggin Hill and visited the RAF station which was one of those most heavily engaged during the Battle of Britain. It was here my brother was based when he was killed. There we toured a memorial chapel, St. George's, dedicated to the memory of the men of that station and my brother's squadron who died in the Battle of Britain. I was disappointed to find that the listing began on 2 June 1940, so my brother's name was not included, he having been killed on 28 May during the British evacuation through Dunkirk.

On a Saturday, my friend's twenty-four-year-old female cousin arrived home from Oxford where she was attending university. The three of us took a bus to Tunbridge Wells to see her brother's school. We toured the buildings and admired its chapel in particular because of its interior beauty, stained glass windows and ivy-covered exterior, the leaves having all turned red. It was our first encounter with an English "public" school and we were surprised at how little liberty the students were allowed. By the time we finished the tour and had met her brother, it was approaching six o'clock and we were stunned to learn that he had to be in his quarters by six p.m., after which the boys were locked in! We were able to have a better visit with him when he came home on Sunday for a few hours.

We were never able to get used to the English eating schedule, which consisted of breakfast, lunch, afternoon tea and dinner. It seemed to us we were always just sitting down to, or getting up from, the table. But our hostess fed us very well and the way she managed it on the wartime rations deserved and got our grateful thanks.

We returned to London, arriving there about noon, and found our lodgings on Lancaster Gate where we had arranged to meet others of our group returning from their leaves. We walked about central London and had our first encounter with a news theatre; that is, a movie house showing nothing but newsreels. That evening we found our way to the Overseas Club where there was dancing. We didn't dance much but spent most of our time gawking at the variety of uniforms and shoulder badges to be seen. I noted those from Belgium, Poland, France, USA, Kenya, British West Indies, Brazil, Australia, New Zealand and, of course, Canada. In addition there was a group of Indian naval officers who wore no distinctive shoulder badges. It certainly convinced us we were involved in a "World War." Returning to our quarters we had our fist experience with the London Underground and were greatly impressed—even though we goofed and went to Paddington, not knowing we could take the "tube" to Lancaster Gate. As a result we had quite a long walk to our hotel.

The next morning we took an early train back to Bournemouth arriving there very hungry as a promised early breakfast at our lodgings failed to materialize. All we had received was a cup of very weak tea which one of us had to drink from a sugar bowl as there weren't enough cups. There hadn't been any sugar in it anyway.

In Bournemouth we returned to the same time-killing routine interspersed with brief moments of meaningful activity. We were issued with RAF flying kit, much of which was "second hand" although in pretty good condition in the main. But one of our group was issued a flying suit which had several small holes in it. They looked suspiciously like bullet holes, at least to our untrained eyes. Also, we were taken out to test our respirators

This test was done by having us don the respirators and walk about in a small building filled with tear gas. If a respirator didn't fit properly it very soon became obvious. Then we were asked to remove the gas masks and take a whiff of tear gas. I was near the door so I took only one very small sniff before dashing out. That was enough. We also had been issued with an impervious gas cape made of a very stiff variety of impregnated cloth, the shoulders of which now were smeared with gas detecting paint. We lugged the respirators around everywhere we went until the straps almost grew into our shoulders. We were each issued with a large shell dressing which we were instructed to carry always in our respirator pouches. Some of us were to find use for them later

There were a few reminders that a war was actually in progress. One morning while parading for roll call in front of the Highcliffe Hotel we were "beaten up" by a Lancaster. It came across the sea toward us with its propeller tips barely clearing the waves and pulled up sharply to roar over our heads, clearing the cliff-top hotel by a bare 50 feet. We assumed it was piloted by an RCAF type who had preceded us through the PRC.

We were warned, too, to beware of tip-and-run raiders. Occasionally a Focke-Wulf 190 would slip across the channel at wave-top height to avoid radar and strafe anything it saw that looked like it might be a worthwhile target. A short time before our arrival, we were told, one raider had strafed the park in which two of our compatriots were walking. One broke left and the other right. The one who ran to the right was killed by machine gun and cannon fire.

Occasionally, while walking in the blackout, we would see searchlights to the east of us in the direction of Southampton and, if the wind was in the right direction, might hear what we took to be the crack of bursting anti-aircraft shells and the crump of bombs. Frequently, during the day we would see formations of American B17 "Flying Fortresses" heading south across the Channel. But what might have been our closest encounter with the war happened in rather amusing circumstances.

Late in our stay at Bournemouth I had purchased a hand-cranked portable phonograph and a few records. One evening some of us were listening to it in our quarters when we began to get objections from the occupants of the room above us in the form of loud banging on the ceiling. In response, one of us stuck his head out the window to shout at our upstairs neighbours to desist. To his surprise he quickly found that the banging was not from upstairs but was the explosions of 40-mm anti-aircraft fire above us. Apparently a tip-and-run raider had sneaked over the town before an air raid alarm could be sounded—or perhaps the authorities thought a single tip-and-run fighter didn't warrant sending the whole town into the air raid shelters.

Our social life at Bournemouth centred mostly on the Pavilion, a combined dance hall and pub on the waterfront near the centre of town. We went frequently and found there was never a shortage of girls with whom to dance. In fact, the girls usually outnumbered the men, practically all of whom were men in uniform and with Canadians from the PRC in the majority.

We soon learned that English girls enjoyed dancing just as much as the girls back home and many of them were very good dancers. A bit of a surprise to us, who had been brought up on the foxtrot, waltz and jive, was the popularity of Latin rhythms in Britain. We had to persuade our English partners to bear with our stumbling efforts to tango and rhumba, but many of them were good and patient teachers. In turn, we taught some of them to jitterbug.

One evening a girl, nicknamed "Babs," was a frequent partner of mine. She was attractive, an excellent dancer and an entertaining companion so I monopolized her for many of the dances. During our conversations she informed me at one point that her father was in the army and was somewhere in the Middle East. After two or three evenings dancing together, she invited me to escort her home. I agreed and was prepared to start out when she informed me she had to wait for her "Mummy." Mummy showed up a short time later, an attractive woman of perhaps forty, escorted by a British army officer, and we began to walk to their home. Although Babs and I lagged behind, and in spite of the darkness of the blackout I could see that Mummy and the army officer were getting very amorously involved and on arrival at the home, they disappeared inside very quickly. Babs invited me in but pleading an early parade in the morning, I demurred. The conduct of the mother raised some rather serious moral doubts in my mind and I couldn't help thinking of the attractive girl in the VD film! Naturally, I have been curious ever since about what would have happened if I had accepted the invitation.

It was only a few days later that several of us were called out while on parade and informed we were being posted to Advanced Flying Units. The friend with whom I had gone on leave and whom I had known since we were in ITS together was posted to Banff in Scotland while I was to go to Church Lawford, near Rugby in the Midlands. We were both devastated as we had become very close. I didn't see him again until many years after the war in Winnipeg, not long before he died.

Aircraftman Second Class Harlo L. Jones while at No. 2 Manning Depot, Brandon, MB, wearing the hated khaki drill summer uniform of the RCAF, which was impossible to keep neatly pressed. The "flying saucer" upper right was actually a lady's windborne hat!

De Havilland Tiger Moths on the line at 6 EFTS, Prince Albert. This photo was taken under different conditions than when the author "enjoyed" flying there in a north Saskatchewan winter. (DND Photo)

The author showing off his flying gear in front of his home in Dinsmore, SK, in January 1943, while on leave after completing Elementary Flying School at Prince Albert. Such clothing was just barely adequate for flying unheated Tiger Moths in the north Saskatchewan winter.

Proof that the author could fly an airplane is provided by photo taken during practice formation at 4 Service Flying Training School, Saskatoon. He is in the left-hand seat of the Cessna Crane. The photo was taken by a fellow student in the formation.

A student pilot practising instrument flying in a Cessna Crane at 4 Service Flying Training School, Saskatoon, in 1943. On his right is "Cec" Raine who was the author's instructor through the Service Flying Training School. Photo by Jones while awaiting his turn "under the hood."

Top left: Newly commissioned 19-year-old Pilot Officer Harlo Jones with his father Luther and mother Hope in front of the United Church in Dinsmore, Saskatchewan. Jones had just received his commission on 30 April 1943 after completing training to wings standard at 4 Service Flying Training School, Saskatoon.

Top right: Ethel Isobel Cloake, my 18-year-old love who, for reasons both altruistic and selfish, I broke up with before going overseas in 1943. Happily the break was mended post-war and we married in 1946.

Right: Propaganda leaflet we dropped offering Germans the choice of repression under Himmler or freedom under Eisenhower. We were convinced the only effect of millions of such leaflets that we dropped was to keep the Germans supplied with toilet paper!

Above: Pilot Officers Clyde Archibald and Harlo Jones clown with guns, overlooking the harbour at Charlottetown, P.E.I. while attending the RAF's 31 General Reconnaissance School in the summer of 1943. 31 GRS was completely manned by English instructors, ground and aircrews.

Left: While on operations we were photographed in nondescript civilian clothes. The photos were printed on paper similar to that used by the Germans for identity photographs. If we were downed and attempted to escape, the Dutch, Belgian or French undergrounds used the photos to forge identity papers for us. I couldn't help wondering if the Jerries would notice we all wore the same tie!

That's me on the right but the important man on the left was my navigator, Don Oldershaw, whose imperturbable manner was a pillar of strength to our whole crew and whose skill as a navigator was demonstrated throughout our tour. Although he was nine years older than me we saw eye-to-eye on everything of importance and shared quarters throughout our tour. I was overjoyed to learn he was awarded the DFC after our tour ended.

Two Canadian aircrew officers look over their planned route for an operation at the navigator's chart table in a Lancaster Mk II. It seems wonderful now that navigators were able to work so accurately in such a confined space, their chart tables almost obscured by electronic equipment. (DND Photo)

"Ok, straighten her out now." It is amazing to recall the amount of manual labour done by wartime ground crews under all weather conditions to prepare aircraft for operations. Here men manhandle a loaded bomb trolley under a Lanc II. After the invasion of Normandy began, aircraft often were bombed up just in time for the armourers to learn that the target, and thus the bomb load, were to be changed. (DND Photo)

Above: The Jerries weren't kidding! Squadron Leader "Jake" Easton brought this Lanc home after a run-in with a Jerry night fighter. It gave us very convincing evidence both of the destructive power of the 20mm cannon which most German fighters had—and of the Lanc's ability to bring us home. (DND Photo)

Opposite top: Hard-working armourers handling thousand-pound bombs in the bomb dump. As novices we shuddered at the casual way they handled high explosive bombs but we soon got used to it, especially after we had a five hundred-pounder or two fall out of the Halifax's wing bomb bays after landing! (DND Photo)

Opposite bottom: Ground crew refuelling a Lancaster Mk II parked on a hardstand where they did all routine maintenance regardless of weather. They didn't get medals but they had the gratitude of air crews whose lives depended on their work. (DND Photo)

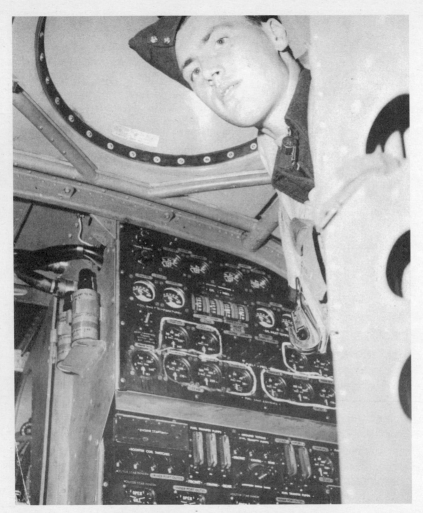

Flight engineer's instrument panel in Halifax Mk VII. Here the FE kept track of all aspects of engine performance and fuel consumption, and acted as lookout with his head in the astrodome. He had a seat beside the pilot but seldom used it except on take-off and landing. Airman unknown. (DND Photo)

My crew with EQ-R. Left to right, Don Oldershaw, navigator, Chatham ON; Harlo "Skipper" Jones, Pilot, Dinsmore SK; Don "Howie" Howard, Wireless Operator, Renfrew ON; Wally Wilkins, Flight Engineer, Montreal PQ; Harold "Happy" or "Hap" Sharpe, Mid-Upper Gunner, Calgary AB; Ralph Syer, Tail Gunner, Hamilton ON; Jean-Pierre "Johnny" Brochu, Bomb Aimer, Montreal PQ.

Mid-upper gunner "Hap" Sharpe and Flight Engineer Wally Wilkins in the "centre rest position" of a Halifax VII. This was occupied by all crew except the pilot, flight engineer and tail gunner during take-off and landing. Other than that, no one ever rested there!

Gunner Ralph Syer in the rear turret of Halifax VII EQ-R. Note the perspex in the centre panel has been removed for better night vision. Syer was a good gunner with a penchant for getting into trouble which resulted in him being the only member of my crew who was not commissioned.

"Hap" Sharpe checking his mid-upper turret on Halifax VII R, "Roger." Gunners liked to check out their guns, turrets and ammo feeds before every operation. God help the armourer who didn't ensure the ammo boxes were full!

Flight Engineer Wally Wilkins on rear-facing folding seat in Halifax VII EQ-R. On take-off he took station beside the pilot to open the throttles fully once the pilot had rudder control and to retract the landing gear and flaps when airborne. Once, due to off-hours over-indulgence in the Sergeants' Mess bar, he got the sequence wrong with almost fatal results for all of us.

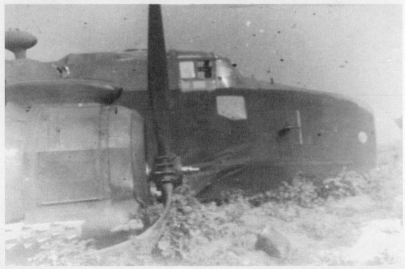

Opposite top:

"O! what a fall was there, my countrymen;
Then I, and you, and all of us fell down."

I remember recalling these lines from Shakespeare as I surveyed the wreckage of Halifax VII NP713 at Eastmoor on 8 August 1944 after a night raid on Caen and a landing during which the brakes failed. I felt it was no great loss as NP713 was a real clunker of an aircraft.

Opposite bottom: Halifax NP713 in the potato patch off the end of the north-south runway at RCAF Station Eastmoor, Yorkshire, with its back visibly broken. It was a "write-off" but without injury to the crew except for the pilot's (yours truly's) sore neck. Several years later I learned two vertebrae in my neck had been broken!

A job that never got finished. I paid a ground crewman to emblazon the nose of our aircraft with, "Roger & Company, Exporters." While I and my crew were on leave another crew managed to prang R-Roger on return from an operation. Although Roger was made serviceable again we finished our tour on other aircraft before it came back. I regret I do not have the names of the ground crewmen on the ladder.

Non-aerodynamic "wing loading," a half ton of aircrew load the starboard wing of our Halifax VII EQ-R "Roger." Standing, left to right, Don Oldershaw, navigator, Chatham ON; Wally Wilkins, flight engineer, Montreal PQ; Don "Howie" Howard, wireless operator, Renfrew ON. Crouching, left to right, Harold "Hap" Sharpe, mid-upper gunner, Calgary AB; Jean-Pierre "Johnny" Brochu, bomb aimer, Montreal PQ; Harlo "Skipper" Jones, pilot, Dinsmore SK; Ralph Syer, rear gunner, Hamilton ON.

This menu represents the finest meal I had in an RAF Mess during the war, and we were grateful the "paddlefeet" let us share it. The day-to-day meals in the same Mess were far below this standard. Happily, on RCAF 6 Group stations the meals were far superior even though made from British military rations. I heard that after the US entered the war the RCAF in Britain was offered American rations which were (to our sorrow) declined.

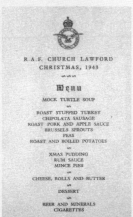

R.A.F. CHURCH LAWFORD
CHRISTMAS, 1943

Menu

MOCK TURTLE SOUP

ROAST STUFFED TURKEY
CHIPOLATA SAUSAGE
ROAST PORK AND APPLE SAUCE
BRUSSELS SPROUTS
PEAS
ROAST AND BOILED POTATOES

XMAS PUDDING
RUM SAUCE
MINCE PIES

CHEESE, ROLLS AND BUTTER

DESSERT

BEER AND MINERALS
CIGARETTES

CHAPTER 9
Advanced Flying Unit

A long with five other commissioned pilots whom I barely knew, I was posted to 18 (P) AFU at RAF Station Church Lawford near Rugby in Warwickshire, effective 2 November 1943 and, as the current saying goes, getting there was half the fun. We made it to Waterloo Station in London and thence to Euston Station and Rugby without difficulty, but on arrival at around 1600 hours there was no transport waiting for us.

We contacted the Railway Transport Officer (RTO) who said he would arrange transport so we settled down to wait. We waited and waited. We purloined a station baggage wagon, piled all our gear on it and after negotiating a long ramp which was not intended for carts, took up a position near the door of the station. To relieve the boredom, we opened up my portable phonograph and got it going, much to the amusement and entertainment of the several hundred people who passed by during the next two hours.

Two of us leaned on the RTO again and this time we waited while he phoned for transport. In about three-quarters of an hour a truck rolled up, its driver saying it was for the six officers so we piled our luggage and ourselves into the back. In a short time we rolled up in front of the Officers' Mess where we unloaded the truck and set off in search of dinner.

We were surprised at how small the Mess was and, on asking an officer who was in the anteroom about dinner, discovered we were at RAF Station Newbold Revel! In a short time the Orderly Officer appeared and called Church Lawford for transport to pick us up. He also organized dinner for us. In the meantime the small group of officers in the Mess were very hospitable, offered us drinks and we conversed quite happily with them. We were unable, however, to discover the function of RAF Station Newbold Revel and decided it was some sort of hush-hush radio or radar station.

We finally arrived at Church Lawford sometime after 11 p.m. and were assigned to billets, two to a room, which were small but quite comfortable. Some sergeant pilots who were to be on our course hadn't arrived in the morning so we were given the day off. My roommate and I unpacked and put everything in order in our quarters, stepped out the door and were informed we had to move. So we packed everything up again.

Our new home was a Nissen hut to which all six of us were assigned. It was located with a few others in a field, outside the confines of the station proper. There were also a couple of small unheated concrete huts each containing four bathtubs in private enclosures—"the ablutions," as they were known to the RAF.

The hut was a miracle of poor construction. It was unlined so its metal walls were constantly cold, always at the same temperature as the outside air. The ends were of poorly finished half-inch wooden boards nailed edge to edge, not tongue-and-groove, and daylight could be seen between many of them. It was approximately 35 feet long by 20 feet wide and contained six beds, six dressers, six small tables, six straight-backed chairs, six small floor mats on the concrete floor, six portable washstands each with enamelled basin, a pail for waste water and a large enamelled pitcher for hot water. In the centre stood one small cylindrical coke-fuelled stove about 14 inches in diameter and 30 inches high—the sole source of heat. A shelf suspended from the curved roof/wall ran the full length of each side and nails had been driven part way into its edges where clothes could be hung. We learned to detest that hut with a vengeance.

As the weather continued to get colder, trying to get the hut warm when we returned to it in the late afternoon was a constant struggle. Each day we were allotted a small bundle of kindling and one pail of coke. Getting the coke to ignite was a hit and miss chore and our kindling was often consumed without success, which sent us foraging the precincts for anything that would burn, including liberal doses of our hard-to-come-by lighter fluid.

We were assigned a cockney batman who usually lit the fire before going off duty in the late afternoon, but frequently his efforts were unsuccessful and we would enter the hut to find the fire out and the stove filled with unconsumed coke and charred kindling. Often our ration of coke was burned up by early evening, but we were able to supplement it clandestinely from the station's supply. A huge pile was stored in a fenced enclosure a short distance away, access to which was gained via an aperture in the fence created by those who had preceded us in our quarters.

The drill on retiring for the night was to fill the stove to the top with stolen coke, then add a pile on top with the stove lid carefully balanced on it so it would slowly settle into position as the coke burned. Often the lid would slide off about the time we got to sleep and hit the concrete floor with a startling clang.

One result of the lack of warmth and the faults in the hut's construction was dampness. Our clothing and bedding were always damp which led us to various expedients in our efforts to get a warm night's sleep. Our bedding consisted of coarse sheets and two heavy grey wool blankets each. These we supplemented by spreading our greatcoats on top and going to bed attired in a "layered look;" pyjamas over our silk and wool flying underwear, wool socks and a wool sweater over all. Even so we shivered through many nights of intermittent sleep.

Part way through the course two of us wound up in hospital with what was diagnosed as "the flu." While there I had a discussion with a sympathetic medical officer about our sleeping attire and he opined that we were defeating ourselves by covering our bodies with so much cold damp clothing and bedding, which was stealing all of our body heat. He suggested we should get into bed naked with only our sheets and blankets. On release from the hospital I tried his prescription and found he was right. I slept cosily after only a short period of warming up and have slept comfortably in the buff ever since. Another use was found for our pyjamas. A few pairs torn into strips were used to plug the cracks in the end walls.

One further word on those huts. Some time after leaving Church Lawford I encountered another RCAF pilot who had done his AFU there. He told me that shortly after we left, the huts were inspected by an RCAF liaison group and were condemned as unfit for human habitation.

Our AFU course began with what was termed "battle training." This consisted of instruction on various mounts for Browning machine guns for use on the ground only, Sten guns, and instruction on throwing hand grenades, all duds. A day or two later we were taken by truck to the Kingsbury range for practice rifle shooting. Our route to the range took us along the highway between Birmingham and Coventry and we were amazed by the heavy traffic on it—practically all big trucks carrying everything from aircraft propellers to pieces of invasion barges. Beside the highway, parked hub to hub, were mile-long lines of armoured personnel carriers and tanks. As all of our travel in England outside of any town up to this time had been by rail, the truck trip along a main highway through some of the industrial countryside was a real eye-opener.

As for the rifle shooting, I remember that on my first five rounds I got two magpies and three bulls and decided that my skills developed shooting gophers on the prairie were still in pretty good condition. However, a day or two later we fired .38 revolvers, after which I decided I had better stick to rifles.

In later battle training sessions we fired Sten guns and Browning machine guns. The Sten, in theory, could be switched to fire either single shots or bursts but it was a roughly manufactured weapon and the ones we used were very unreliable. During one session when one of our group was to fire single shots from the waist, the gun "ran away" and he turned to ask the instructor what was wrong, bringing the still firing gun around with him! Those of us watching hit the deck in record time, throwing ourselves prone on the muddy ground. Fortunately, the weapon had emptied its magazine before its muzzle came to bear on us.

The training aircraft at the AFU was the Airspeed Oxford, a twin-engine aircraft with Armstrong Siddeley Cheetah seven-cylinder radial air-cooled engines of 350 horsepower. On one of our first days off, we walked around the perimeter of the airfield to the downwind end of a runway in use to watch the aircraft landing. We were struck by the long, flat power-on approaches being used which were in sharp contrast to the steeper practically powerless gliding approaches we had been taught during our training in Canada. These looked more like the precautionary landing approaches we had been taught for getting into small fields in emergencies.

Our course proper began with ground school. This, physically, was a disaster. The rough classrooms were graced with the same 14-inch stoves as our Nissen hut, but they were seldom lit. As a result we sat through classes in our greatcoats, knitted scarves and gloves, and by the end of each day were chilled to the bone.

On one occasion when there was a fire in our classroom stove we sat huddled to it as closely as we could, so close that I scorched the lower left corner of my greatcoat which dangled too near the open draft door of the stove. It was not a situation conducive to learning, which is borne out by the fact that I remember absolutely nothing of what we supposedly studied there. All I can recall is the discomfort which went on day after day.

However, we did gain an acquaintance with *Pilots' Notes for the Oxford* and warnings about the various hazards we might encounter while flying in the area. One, in particular, was the clump of 880-foot-high radio masts of the BBC's overseas service clustered in a group of about a dozen not far outside our circuit area.

Often the Mess was not much warmer than our classrooms. The anteroom contained a large fireplace with a tight circle of leather easy chairs around it. Most often by the time we returned from classes and, later in the course, from our flight dispersal sites, the chairs were occupied by those we termed "paddlefeet," the ground staff officers, male and female, who got to the mess for tea before we were free and who erected an invisible and impenetrable wall about themselves.

Usually, if there were any "goodies" for tea they were mostly consumed before our arrival as well. When we complained of the cold we were often chided with the assertion that as Canadians, we should be used to cold. Our standard reply was that Canadians had enough sense to leave the cold outdoors.

It was in the AFU Mess that we first honed our skills on the standard English pub games—darts, to which we soon became addicted, and "shove ha'penny." The latter game unlike darts has not migrated to this country. It was played on a polished board with half-penny coins, one side of which had been flattened and made almost perfectly smooth. And woe betide the careless individual who set a beer glass on the board! We divided our off duty hours between these and either billiards or snooker, and always with a penny or shilling wagered on the outcome—although gambling in the mess was a no-no.

There was also an electric radio-phonograph and we used to bring our records over and play them over and over again, often to the intense disgust of some of the older and more staid senior officers.

Some of our records resulted from a fortuitous incident in a record shop in Rugby. A friend and I had gone in looking for, primarily, swing records. The shop's owner rather disdainfully stated he didn't carry trash like that but then suggested we come into a back room where he thought there were some records he had got by mistake.

He directed us to a small stack and we proceeded to examine them, ending up tossing coins to see who would get which ones. I picked up the Mills Brothers' version of "Glowworm" and several records featuring Lena Horne with the Chamber Music Society of Lower Basin Street on numbers such as "Careless Love" and "Basin Street Blues," as well as Dinah Shore's "Something to Remember You By," the last a real heart jerker in our situation. I have often wondered since if the shop owner actually catered somewhat clandestinely to the musical tastes of some of Rugby's famed boys' school pupils.

Three weeks after arrival at AFU we finally got airborne. Our first flight was as passengers in an Avro Anson, intended to show us the lay of the land and handy landmarks as well as some of the hazards such as the radio masts. It was a dead loss for its intended purpose but it certainly exposed us to what was probably the greatest hazard to flying in the midlands—industrial haze. From 1500 feet above ground the slant visibility was so bad we could see absolutely nothing on the ground and vertical visibility wasn't much better.

After deciding that the exercise was useless the pilot, a senior instructor, set course from a familiar landmark and we tracked right over the aerodrome. He let down and turned to join the circuit. We were unable to find the airport again! Fortunately, there was a wireless operator in the crew for just such an eventuality. He got a QDM (radio bearing) which took us back to the airport and this time the pilot managed to do a circuit without losing sight of the field. Needless to say, it was a very tight circuit and required a very steep approach to the landing with generous use of the brakes to keep from going off the end of the runway. That was our initiation to flying in England.

We were issued helmets with radio earphones and oxygen masks with microphones and were introduced to radio procedures, a new experience for us. Our previous flying had been done without benefit of voice communication with the ground. We were assigned to flights and taken to their dispersed locations around the field where we found flight rooms that were little more than shacks and two or three Nissen-type shelters for aircraft. These were open-ended and just wide enough to cover the nose and engines of the aircraft, leaving wings, most of the fuselages and tails outside. They provided a small amount of shelter for the groundcrews working on the planes.

I still have a profound admiration for those groundcrew "erks," as they were called by the RAF. Their working conditions in the winter were unbearably cold and it seemed their coveralls and sleeveless leather jackets were barely adequate for the conditions. And there were never enough of the jackets for every airman to have one. But they carried on magnificently with great good humour.

Starting the aircraft engines was one of their coldest trials. The Cheetah engines were hand cranked which meant an airman had to get up on the wing, open a flap on the side of the nacelle, insert a hand crank and crouch there, shivering, until a pilot went through his pre-startup checks and called "Contact" through his open side window. The airman then operated the crank, usually bare-handed as the RAF didn't issue gloves, straining to turn the engine over until it fired and started up. Then he was blasted with the icy slipstream from the propeller as the pilot goosed the engine to keep it running. If it stopped the process had to be repeated. The groundcrew man then had to remove the crank, close and lock the nacelle flap, and crawl up on the other wing to start the second engine.

It was not uncommon for the airman to ask the pilot for a penny to turn the slotted head of the locking screw on the nacelle flap and it was customary for them to "forget" to return it. Considering RAF ground-crew pay, I'm sure none of us begrudged them their little swindle. They certainly earned those pennies.

We learned though never to leave a package of our Canadian cig-arettes in the flight room. They disappeared almost magically. By contrast, there was a brand of English cigarette that not even the erks would bother stealing. On foggy mornings when there was still no aerial activity we took a shortcut to flights by riding our bicycles down the main runway. One morning as I cycled to flights I felt a slight bump. I stopped to investigate and found I had run over an unopened package of Wild Woodbine cigarettes. I pocketed them and later placed them on a window sill in the flight room. When we were posted away some weeks later they were still there. No one would even steal them. I was left wondering who had bought them in the first place.

If we encountered things like stones while riding on the runway we would stop and toss them off, as they could cause a tire failure on land-ing by cutting the tire.

Our turn to work outside on the aircraft came when flying was washed out due to weather conditions. Then we were detailed to swing compasses on the aircraft. An aircraft was towed to a compass rose painted on the asphalt surface of a dispersal site and there placed on various true headings while compass deviation was corrected as much as possible in a complex drill. Final errors were noted, and a deviation card completed showing the corrections to be applied to it mentally by a pilot when flying the airplane on various headings. The card was placed in a special holder on the instrument panel of the plane. When swinging compasses we didn't "swing the lead" as our lives might depend on the accuracy of the compass and its deviation card.

Another chilly job we each had at least once during the course was to be detailed as aerodrome control pilot. This meant spending the better part of a morning, afternoon or night at the downwind end of the runway in use, ensconced in a tiny wheeled shack without heat and equipped with an Aldis lamp with a red lens.

The principal duty was to watch each aircraft on final approach to make sure it had its undercarriage down. If not, it was given a red light by the control pilot's Aldis lamp which was the signal for it to overshoot and go round again. I drew this detail once and shivered through a damp, cold morning on the end of the runway without even the excitement of having to signal off a single aircraft.

One member of our course, returning from a night cross-country on a dark rainy night, was so happy to find the drome after searching for it for some time in the miserable weather conditions, he bored straight in and landed with his wheels up. He either missed the signal or ignored it, or perhaps the control pilot hadn't been able to see whether or not the wheels were down. After the aircraft had ground to a stop on its belly the pilot climbed out, dragging his parachute, and scurried some distance away before he stopped, turned, and yelled "Shut up, you silly bastard!" at the still-blaring undercarriage warning horn.

Our first flying experience on the Oxford was a bit of a shock to us. First, the aircraft was considerably bigger than the Cessna Cranes we had flown at SFTS and was over a ton heavier. Secondly, its handling characteristics were much heavier than the Crane's which could be flown with a very light touch. On our first dual circuits and landings we learned the reason for the long flat approaches we had commented on shortly after our arrival. The Oxford was no glider! Without power it had a remarkably high rate of descent so we no longer did the gliding approaches we had been taught in Canada.

Rather our normal landings now approached the precautionary landing drill we had been taught there.

Another new worry for us was the aircraft's air brakes. Directional braking was governed by the rudder pedals but braking intensity was provided by squeezing a control lever on the pilot's control column wheel, not by toe pressure on the rudder pedals. And we were warned to keep an eye on the air pressure gauge. Over-use of the brakes could exhaust the air pressure faster than the aircraft's pump could replace it, resulting in total failure of the brakes. We were to find later that this system was used on all of the English aircraft we flew and I recall a group of Canadians on one occasion jokingly composing a letter to the Air Ministry informing them of a wonderful North American invention—the hydraulic brake.

Although the Oxford was somewhat stiff on the controls, we adapted to it without much difficulty. After signing certificates that we had been instructed in and understood the petrol, oil, ignition, brake and hydraulic systems, action in event of fire and method of abandoning the Oxford aircraft, we were allowed to fly solo.

When the weather was decent we were able to get a good look at the surrounding country and note landmarks, such as Warwick Castle. There was one particularly high brick or stone smokestack of awesome proportions which always emitted a prodigious quantity of smoke. After recognizing it, we could always find the airfield by following the cant phrase taught by our instructors, "Steer oh-four-oh from Smoky Joe." We toured by air the places we had heard of many times such as Stratford-on-Avon and war-ravaged Coventry.

Frequently in the mornings the aircraft parked outside were covered with a thin coat of frost. We were warned never, never to attempt to take the Oxford off with even the lightest coating of frost on the wings. It just wouldn't fly! While we were at Church Lawford, untold quantities of glycol were used to clear the aircraft of frost on many mornings.

Our dual instruction continued with hours spent on single-engine turning and landing, overshooting, taking off and going around again on instruments, turns without power, engine failure during and after take-off, all the various attitudes and manoeuvres of which the aircraft was capable. We also learned some bits of aircraft handling such as flying at a constant height with various power settings thus changing airspeed without gain or loss of altitude. At last we were tested on our "needle, ball and airspeed" flying; that is, flying without instruments except the turn and bank and airspeed indicators, and instrument flying on one engine, after which we were pronounced ready for night flying.

Some dual "instruction" verged on the idiotic. One day I was assigned to some form of practice flying with an English sergeant-pilot instructor. After only a few minutes in the air he directed me to a rather small grassed emergency field where he took over and landed. He taxied up to a single small building on the field, locked the brakes, set the throttles up almost to cruising boost and revs and climbed out of the plane, summoning me to follow him. In shocked disbelief I did, and accompanied him to the shack where there were three or four airmen huddled around a stove. He took a couple of mugs from a shelf and poured two cups of tea. After giving me one, he settled himself comfortably into a chair and lit a cigarette inviting me to do the same. After a half hour or so in conversation with the airmen in which I took little part, we went back out to the aircraft and flew back to Church Lawford. The point in setting the throttles while on the ground was to burn up enough fuel so it would appear we had been airborne all the while. I couldn't help but think of the seamen who most probably had given their lives to get that avgas to England.

Before beginning night flying there was one new stage to be completed—Beam Approach Training, or "BAT Flight" as it was termed. We were posted to 1533 BAT Flight which operated from the same air-field but had its own dispersal site and aircraft. Here we were introduced to "day/night" flying which was night flying in the daytime. This was accomplished by the student wearing special goggles that obliterated almost everything but the specially illuminated aircraft instruments and by the use of special (I believe sodium) lights along the runway. We learned the details of beam flying with such procedures as identifying the beam, measuring the beam to find which direction to go along it to its point of origin and making beam approaches and landings. This course was all dual and for me comprised a total of seventeen hours and fifteen minutes flying time in twelve days. I was assessed as having a "good knowledge of beam approach procedures" and "flying quite satisfactory." Not once in my subsequent wartime career did I have to use a beam approach.

I recall one incident in particular while on BAT Flight. One of the instructors, a Squadron Leader, one day left his log book in the flight room. First we noticed it was marked "Volume 2" and on examining it further decided that he had flown just about every type of aircraft in the RAF for the preceding twenty or more years. I would have liked dearly to have seen Volume 1. It occurred to me to wonder, too, if he had left it there just to impress us. If that was his motive, he certainly succeeded.

Back in the AFU flights, we plunged immediately into night flying which lasted for most of the balance of the course. This included all of the daytime aircraft manoeuvres plus several cross-country flights of up to two and one-half hours' duration, often in miserable weather conditions. And it was during this phase of the course that we lost one of the members of our Nissen hut sextet.

On a solo night cross-country flight in rainy weather he ploughed into the bracing cables of the BBC radio masts six hundred feet up. It was decided he had caught a cable inboard of one of the engines which had thrown the aircraft into a flat spin. He was quite a heavy man and the impact on hitting the ground had broken his back. There was no fire and somehow, God only knows how, he had pulled himself out of the aircraft and several yards along the ground before he died. The Oxford was a notoriously difficult aircraft to get out of in an emergency. He had to get between the two pilots' seats, over the wing spars, and back to the fuselage door aft of the trailing edge of the wing, and then open a badly damaged door.

Six NCO pilots from our course acted as pall bearers at his funeral while we officers attended as honourary pall bearers. But one riddle remained. The NCOs declared afterward that the coffin wasn't heavy enough to have contained his body. To this assertion there was no answer, and it troubles me even now.

We speculated often on what had caused him to collide with the masts. They were equipped, as were barrage balloons, with very short-range radio beepers which we could hear on our R/T sets. As one approached their sound became louder, giving an indication that one was headed toward them. They were turned off only when there was threat of enemy air action, and there hadn't been any on the night our friend was killed. We could only assume that when he heard the sound, he was very close to the masts and flying past them. He must have turned the wrong way in his effort to avoid them and hit the cables before being able to detect that the sound was again getting louder.

But before this tragedy there had been some happier times: Christmas, my twentieth birthday on December 29 and New Year's all came about halfway through the course. On Christmas Eve we cycled in to Rugby and toured the pubs, winding up at the Saracen's Head and finally the Grand. Here we got involved in playing darts for beers with some of the older regulars. We soon learned that one doesn't take on some of those oldsters without first observing their skill. We were soundly beaten time after time, much to the detriment of our purses.

We finally made our way homeward. I was in the lead shortly after leaving the pub and after cycling a block or so I couldn't hear my companion following and began to make a U-turn in the middle of the street—and collided with him! We both went down in a tangle of arms, legs and bicycles from which we extracted ourselves with some difficulty, but made it the rest of the way back without further incident. One of our hut-mates was not so fortunate.

When cycling from Rugby in the blackout we watched for the dark shape of our Nissen hut and just past it made a left turn onto a road leading to the huts. Our mate had done the same thing but had mistaken a straw stack for the hut and turned into a deep ditch filled with water. He was still hanging his clothes up to dry when we returned.

In the mess we were served a Christmas dinner that was the finest meal I had in an RAF Mess all the time I was overseas. I still have a copy of the printed menu in my album. It began with mock turtle soup, proceeded to roast stuffed turkey, chipolata sausage, roast pork with apple sauce, peas, boiled and baked potatoes (as well as the inevitable brussels sprouts) and concluded with mince pies and Christmas pudding with rum sauce, and finally cheese with rolls and butter, beer, mineral waters and cigarettes. Considering the average calibre of food in the mess, that dinner was almost a miracle.

Christmas Day had been a hectic one. It began with a "gift breakfast"—one fresh egg each! This was a happy change from the watery powdered eggs of our more usual fare. The day was spent in traditional ways with the station's officers serving the noontime meal to the airmen and a delegation of officers proceeding to the sergeant's mess to invite them to ours. This turned into a roaring party and it was later reported that we and our guests did away with 57 imperial gallons of beer in little more than an hour. It must be remembered, however, that British wartime draught beer was pretty weak stuff.

As student pilots we were surprised at the conduct of some of our usually stern instructors. One Flight Lieutenant had somehow obtained a bottle of scotch which he was well into by the time the sergeants arrived, supplementing each swig from the bottle with a beer chaser. At one point he decided to lead a singsong and to do so sat on the headrest of one of the big easy chairs, his feet on the seat, while a companion, another instructor, braced him there. Unfortunately for him someone called to the second instructor who, distracted, turned around and let go of the conductor. The next sound heard was a dull thud as our song leader tumbled backwards and disappeared behind the piano where he remained in blissful sleep for a couple of hours before reviving and taking up again right where he had left off!

The day ended with an ENSA (Entertainments National Services Association) concert in the station cinema. The comedy was pretty lewd in places, and we were surprised at the audience reaction—the broader sallies got a much bigger reaction and more laughter from the Wafs than from the men. The only quip I remember was made by a baggy-trousered comic who parodied an officer instructing the troops that 'pee-low' is merely the French pronunciation of pilot and makes no reference whatsoever to the ablutions.

On New Year's Eve a dance was staged in the mess with a couple of bus loads of volunteer girls imported from Rugby for the evening. I managed to attract the attention of a stunningly beautiful girl in a body-hugging black lace evening dress. Evening dresses were a rarity in wartime Britain. She was a marvellous dancer and had a very attractive and lively personality. We got along famously and I usurped her attention for most of the evening.

When the dance ended I joined her on the bus back to Rugby where she had checked into one of the small hotels as she actually lived in Coventry. I parted company with her at the hotel door after making a date for a week or two later. I then walked back to the RAF station, a distance of about three miles, arriving at our Nissen hut around 3:30 a.m. chilled and weary. The next day the weather was fine and we had to fly but I managed to survive.

When the time for my date with my New Year's Eve girlfriend arrived we were in the midst of night flying but I arranged with my flight commander to have that night off. I had been up flying the previous night and had spent the day writing letters and getting my uniform all tiddly in preparation for our meeting. As she worked at the B.T.H. factory in Rugby we met at a pub when she got off work in the late afternoon, had an early dinner in a restaurant and went to a movie. After the movie we again hit one of the pubs and chatted for an hour or so. She told me some of her background and of her experiences as an air raid warden in Hull during the Blitz.

One incident she recounted showed the capriciousness of high explosive bomb blasts. While she patrolled the streets with a male companion during a raid a bomb exploded nearby. The blast lifted her over a wall and dumped her, unhurt, into someone's back garden. She made her way back to the street and found her companion where they had been standing before the explosion. He was dead.

We became so involved in our conversation we lost track of the hour until we realized suddenly it was almost time for her train to Coventry. We made a frantic dash to the station but arrived too late. Her train had gone. We were nonplussed but I decided the only thing I could do was to try to find her a hotel room. We went to a small commercial hotel in the centre of Rugby and rang the bell. Fortunately, they had rooms available and we were invited in. As I didn't have to be back on the station until late the next afternoon I booked a second room for myself and we went to the hotel's sitting room where there was a good fire in the fireplace.

As residents of the hotel we were allowed to order drinks although it was now after normal pub hours. In a few minutes we were comfortably ensconced on a carpet in front of the fireplace with thick chair cushions under our heads and a couple of gin-and-limes close at hand. We were alone in the room.

We chatted for a while as we enjoyed our drinks and then decided it was time to retire. I escorted her to the door of her room and readily accepted her invitation to come in. It wasn't long before we decided to go to bed and as she disrobed I stripped to my shorts and got into a warm soft double bed. I watched as she stripped to panties and bra in which she was provocatively beautiful. Then she slipped into her coat to go down the hall to the loo. While she was gone the warmth of the bed, the gin, and my previous forty or so hours without sleep caught up with me. I have a very hazy recollection of her warm body curled around my back spoon fashion as I fell into a deep sleep. When I awoke in the morning she was gone.

A short time later a group of us went to a pub in the village of Old Bilton, a sort of suburb of Rugby, and the closest pub to our quarters. We reached it by walking across muddy fields to a highway into the town. I was surprised to see her sitting there with a girlfriend and was a little concerned about what her attitude toward me might be. However, she greeted me with the same warmth she had shown on our previous meetings and informed me that she had that day moved into digs in Old Bilton to be closer to her work. We chatted until closing time and I accompanied her to her door where she apologized for not being able to invite me in as her suite was still in disarray.

I returned to the station walking on air with visions of a beautiful liaison dancing in my mind. I was sure we were falling in love. The next day my group was posted to an Operational Training Unit.

In the rush of getting our log books up to date and signed, doing the rounds to get cleared from all of the station's working sections and getting our effects packed for the move I didn't have time for another visit to Old Bilton before leaving the next day. I didn't even have her address and I never saw her again.

War *is* hell!

CHAPTER 10

Operational Training Unit

We were taken to 22 OTU by truck, as it was not far from Church Lawford to Wellesbourne Mountford. Our first three weeks were spent on the ground and the first major step was forming crews. This was something in the order of a pandemonium exercise, as none of the pilots had ever met any of those of the other aircrew trades from which our crews were to be made up. It was accomplished by putting us all in one big room with a barrel of beer and good luck wishes from the OTU staff.

I was at somewhat of a loss how to proceed but upon looking around the room I spotted a man wearing a navigator's wing sitting quietly amid the turmoil. He was quite a big man and looked to be a little older than most of us. He was holding a pint of beer but had scarcely sipped on it. I approached him and asked if he would like to crew up with me. He assented readily and we exchanged names. He was Don Oldershaw and he hailed from Chatham, Ontario. We chatted for a moment before being approached by a bomb aimer, a rather nice looking man who appeared to be twenty-one or twenty-two years old, and we accepted his offer to join us. Within a few minutes we had acquired a wireless operator, Don Howard, from Renfrew, Ontario, and as we stood chatting two rather diminutive but sturdy men approached us, one about five feet six inches tall and the other an inch or so shorter. They were to become our two air gunners, Harold Sharpe from Calgary, and Ralph Syer of Hamilton.

We spent the rest of the afternoon getting acquainted and I was quite happy with the way everything had worked out. I communicated the names of our group to an OTU officer who was there for the purpose and we were officially a crew. Meanwhile, the other fifty or so types in the room had similarly sorted themselves out. It was a strange experience but it seemed to work out well for most of us. The flaws didn't appear until later.

Oldershaw and I were the only commissioned officers among the six of us while the remaining four were sergeants. When we were moved from Wellesbourne to a satellite field at Gaydon for our OTU flying, Don and I shared a room in the quarters as we did for the balance of our time together, a total of about nine months. I found him pleasant, dependable, quiet, sober and a good companion who always seemed to have some project on the go, such as taking photographs and developing them himself. He used the blackout curtains in bathrooms to create darkrooms.

When we were in a town together he was always on the lookout for films, which were very scarce, or purchasing strangely-named chemicals from pharmacy shops. When we were socializing with the rest of the crew, he could make a half-pint of beer last for hours. He didn't smoke either, which at times worked out to my benefit as occasionally, someone who didn't know he was a non-smoker or some benevolent organization would send him cigarettes which he passed on to me. At that time people could send them overseas at a cost of one dollar for 300—shipping included!

Our first two or three weeks at OTU were spent on the ground being familiarized with all of the intricacies of the Vickers Wellington bomber on which we were to do our flying. We did innumerable practice drills ranging from the pilot's cockpit checks to abandoning the aircraft in event of fire or some other catastrophe. We were also given parachute practice, not from the air but by sliding down a cable from the top of a hangar wall to tumbling mats laid out on the floor. We were told, for example, always to release the parachute harness just before hitting the water if we had to jump into the sea so as not to become entangled in the shroud lines. This we did in the hangar, hitting the quick release box on the 'chute harness just before our feet hit the mats and then somersaulting forward in the approved method for landing on the ground.

We were also given a dozen lessons on rubber dinghies. These included being taken to a swimming pool in the town of Leamington Spa where we were taught to inflate circular dinghies, how to hold a whole crew, how to bring them to full inflation with an accordion-style pump, to right dinghies that had inflated upside down, and how to paddle them correctly so they didn't just go around in endless circles. For these exercises, we stripped to our shorts and donned full flying gear with parachute harness and mae west.

The rub was unless you were the first crew of the day you had to don gear which had just been taken off by the crew preceding you. Pulling on a soaking wet and chilled canvas flying suit was far from a pleasant experience. I found it less unpleasant to take the flying suit into the pool with me and put it on in the water.

It was during these first days together as a crew that we sorted one another out by names. I began to answer to "Skipper." Don Oldershaw retained his name but Don Howard became "Howie" while Harold Sharpe, because of his good-humoured wide grin was tagged "Happy" after the dwarf in the Disney movie *Snow White and the Seven Dwarfs;* this name was soon shortened to "Hap." Ralph Syer remained Ralph and he was to become the worrisome one of the crew, with a chip constantly on his shoulder and a very pugnacious personality although he could, when he wished, be very pleasant and congenial.

Our flying began in earnest on 15 March and was considerably more intense than at AFU. I logged 10 hours and 50 minutes in the first ten days of flying, mostly dual and solo "circuits and bumps." This must have been a real trial for the rest of the crew because they had nothing to do but ride along and listen to the instructor chide me for any errors I made—errors which might have a disastrous affect on their immediate futures.

I found the Vickers Wellington Mk III quite an easy airplane to fly. With its two 1,375 horsepower Bristol Hercules 14-cylinder twin-row radial sleeve-valve engines, it had bags of power for our type of flying which seldom involved a really heavy load. It did seem big though, with its 86-foot wingspan and empty weight of nine and a quarter tons.

One of the most remarkable things about the Wellington from a pilot's point of view was the pilot's seat. I am sure it was the most comfortable ever put into an airplane, at least until well after the war. It was deeply padded, leather-covered, fully adjustable and positively luxurious. The greatest risk associated with it was that of falling asleep on a long trip although it never happened to me. On the other hand, there was a risk associated with the pilot's location. A side window beside him could be slid open but one didn't try to wave one's hand outside it. The tips of the whirling propeller blades on the port engine flashed past it at a distance of about ten inches directly in line with the pilot's head.

The only problem I encountered with the "Wimpy," as the aircraft was affectionately known, was on final approach when full flap was selected. As the flaps went down, the nose of the aircraft came up and it was necessary to restrain this tendency while cranking on nose-down trim. At my weight, which hadn't increased much since my enlistment, I found it almost impossible to hold the nose down with my left arm while trimming the aircraft with my right. I solved this problem by tucking my left elbow inside the big hook on the left side of my parachute chest-pack harness. Thus braced against my chest my forearm became a locking bar between me and the control column, preventing it from moving back.

On 25 March we took off with an instructor as captain of our aircraft along with a second trainee crew and instructor in another airplane. The object of the trip was a sea search to try to find a Bomber Command aircraft or its crew who had radioed they were ditching their shot-up airplane on return from Germany. We went out over the sea to the approximate location of the last fix obtained on it and began a creeping line-ahead search, with the second Wimpy in the lead and us slightly behind and to their right.

The visibility was so bad in industrial haze that our two aircraft were almost in formation while flying at a half visibility distance apart and about a hundred feet above the water. Above that height we couldn't even see the surface of the water except directly below us. At the end of each long leg of the search, they gave us a flash from an Aldis lamp to let us know they were going to begin a turn as we were maintaining radio silence—but once they forgot. As we watched for the signal they suddenly began a turn to starboard right in front of us. We dived almost to the sea and passed beneath them but their trailing antenna took off our fixed antenna which ran from a short post just behind the cockpit to the rudder fin, while our trailing antenna was torn off when its weighted end hit the sea. They also lost their trailing antenna.

There were hot words exchanged between the two instructors after we landed. Altogether we were out on the search for five and a half hours but saw nothing in spite of all of the members of both crews carefully scanning the sea surface, or what we could see of it. I never learned if the ditched crew ever was found but it is highly unlikely.

The next day our bomb aimer voluntarily went LMF (Lack of Moral Fibre) as the service called it or, as we termed it, "Lack of Guts."

In other words, he requested that he be taken off flying duties and disappeared from our ken almost immediately. I have no idea what became of him.

During the next four or five days we flew more than twenty-one hours with an assortment of bomb aimers up front. Then we were assigned another to complete our crew and drew a veritable jewel. He was Jean Pierre Bernard Brochu from Montreal, who became affectionately known to us as "Johnny." He had been one of a French-Canadian crew destined for the Alouette (425) Squadron but his crew had been wiped out in a crash while he was in hospital with the flu.

When he joined us his English was quite broken but I never ceased to be amazed at how quickly he assumed our speech—and not just our argot. By reading extensively he soon had an English vocabulary that exceeded those of some of the other crew members who had grown up speaking the language. He had a marvellous sense of humour and fitted in almost at once. I admit to a certain hesitation about accepting him, mostly because of the unknown attitudes of the rest of the crew, but my concerns disappeared with our first flights and practice bombing exercises. Soon we all thought the world of him. Occasionally he was joshed but he gave back as good as he got—in spades!

Soon we were into flying at quite a heavy pace—circuits and landings day and night, practice bombing, fighter affiliation, air-to-air firing with the gunners shooting at a towed drogue, and cross-county flights of up to five and one half hours duration. During these long flights we travelled the length and breadth of Great Britain as training for our navigators and wireless operators. Fighter affiliation exercises were always done in daylight with a Tomahawk or Hurricane making dummy attacks on us while our gunners practised their running commentary to the pilot and called for the "corkscrew" manoeuvre that was the standard Bomber Command evasive tactic.

This manoeuvre involved a sharp diving turn toward the direction from which the fighter was attacking, then rolling out and climbing in the opposite direction. The object was to increase as much as possible the angle of deflection a fighter would have to allow when attacking, making a miss more likely and, at night, hopefully eluding the fighter in the process. The gunners also used camera guns, the film from which later was used to assess the effectiveness of their defensive firing. Both Hap and Ralph were rated highly. One of their favourite tricks when bored with practice firing was to aim at the drogue tow cable and cut it, thus ending the exercise while the drogue drifted slowly to the ground, trailing behind the remaining piece of heavy cable.

During our final five days of flying at OTU, we made our first incursion into enemy territory. On 25 April 1944 we flew a night "Nickel Raid" into France. Its objective was to drop propaganda leaflets on Paris. Our course took us close to Rouen and to allow for the wind we dropped our leaflets about 60 miles northwest of the target city. We encountered our first flak on this trip but it was slight and scattered as we didn't fly over any heavily defended areas. One of the participating aircraft didn't return but we don't know what happened to it. We contended that the sole result of these raids was to keep Europe supplied with toilet paper, known colloquially as "bumph."

Two nights later we took part in a "Bullseye." This was a diversionary raid intended to draw German fighters away from the main bomber force that was to go in a few minutes later and by a much different route. We went out over the North Sea in company with a host of aircraft from several OTU's simulating a bomber stream. We flew to a position north of the Frisian Islands and then turned southeast as if heading for Kiel or Hamburg. At 6 degrees, 30 minutes east longitude we reversed direction and headed for England. Again, we never learned how successful our ruse was.

One thing I did learn on that sortie was that I had a damn good navigator. Out over the sea there was no way of finding wind direction or strength so we began by using the "met winds," as we called those predicted by the meteorologists at pre-flight briefing. As we flew over the sea Don began taking star shots with the sextant which indicated we were drifting north of track. In this he was assisted by Johnny who with Don's help had taught himself to use the sextant. Soon Don informed me that the met winds were "all to cock" and began giving me courses to steer based on his star shots which were corroborated by Johnny's. A day or two later I was informed by the OTU navigation leader that when all the navigators' logs were back plotted, we had travelled closer to the desired track than any of the other dozens of crews on the trip.

Bombing was practised both by day and night with Johnny using the old Mark VII bomb sight to aim eleven and a half pound practice bombs that were so small they looked almost ridiculous in the gaping bomb bay of the Wimpy. As this bomb sight could not compensate for any change in the aircraft's attitude all of our bombing was done while flying straight and level. Fortunately, by the time we got to a squadron the new Mk XIV sight was standard in Bomber Command, permitting some climb, dive or turn while bombing. This sight used one of the first rudimentary analog computers to compensate for changes in the aircraft's attitude, airspeed, wind direction and velocity, and the ballistic characteristics of the bombs being dropped.

But our adventures didn't all take place in the air. At Gaydon our quarters were on top of a hill on a road slanting downward at a steep angle. We cycled to and from our quarters, coasting down the hill and braking near the bottom to make a turn leading to the gate of the station proper. One chilly morning we coasted down the hill but when I applied the brakes near the bottom, nothing happened and moments later I found myself lying on the grass on the verge of the road with the bike on top of me. I wasn't injured but I learned from that how ineffective the rubber block brakes were when the wheel rims were coated with icy frost, quite unlike the enclosed Canadian coaster brakes we were used to.

On the OTU training staff there was one particularly bad-tempered Squadron Leader, a Canadian, and I never saw him in a good mood. One morning I had just picked up my food from the steam table in the mess dining room and was whistling softly as I looked around for a place to sit. I started off in the direction of a table at which a Squadron Leader whom I had not met was sitting alone. While I was still some distance from the table he suddenly barked, "Stop that goddam whistling!" I stopped, startled, and abruptly altered course 90 degrees to another table.

A few days later four or five of us were walking along one of the station's streets clad in our raincoats which bore no rank marks. We encountered this same Squadron Leader, also in his raincoat, and passed him by without saluting. A few paces later we were checked by his angry shout and stood still while he gave us a profane dressing down for failing to salute. Finished, he turned and began to walk away when one of our number shouted, "You! Come back here!" and began to peel off his raincoat. He was a Wing Commander who had come from Training Command in Canada and was taking the same course as the rest of us. He gave the Squadron Leader a short but very sharp lecture on good manners among officers and then dismissed him—after having been saluted properly. The rest of us, all junior officers, didn't try to hide our smiles of satisfaction at this turn of events as we had all had some sort of run-in with this type and his reputation for surliness was known to all.

For trainees, who seemed always to be undergoing some form of castigation from our mentors, any mishap on their part gave us added hope that we weren't just bumbling clots. We savoured one incident in particular. One of our group on landing a Wellington went off the edge of the runway and one main wheel became hopelessly mired almost to the hub in the winter mud that was common to most RAF fields. This blocked the runway in use necessitating a delay in most flying and landings until the runway was changed.

The Wing Commander Chief Flying Instructor, witnessing this, jumped into the first car available, which happened to be the Commanding Officer's, and raced out to the aircraft. The aircrew opened the hatch under the nose of the Wimpy and dropped the ladder. He climbed up, pushed the pilot aside and began ramming one throttle wide open in bursts in an attempt to dislodge the stuck wheel. Suddenly, with one engine roaring, the wheel came loose and the tail swung around-until one side of the tail plane whacked the CO's car, doing considerable damage to both. It did our morale good to know that P/O Prune-type accidents could happen to the best. This one surely qualified the CFI for the "Most Highly Derogatory Order of the Irremovable Finger," awarded in Training Memoranda to the perpetrators of such boners.

There was one occasion, however, when most of us truly felt sorry for the CFI. The occasion was a CO's parade which I believe was the only one held during our time at OTU. The Wingco was parade commander and when the parade was formed up he took command and awaited the arrival of the CO. As the CO approached, he turned to face us and call the parade to attention. Sadly, he had a stammer and try as he might, he couldn't get the order out. He made several stuttering attempts but his vocal apparatus refused to cooperate. In desperation he turned to his adjutant who gave the order. As he was well liked by most of us, it tore at our hearts to see him so embarrassed but, as usual, one or two unfeeling clots laughed.

The mud on the airfields of Britain in winter was a constant trial and not just to the aircraft. It seemed impossible to walk anywhere without getting shoes loaded with the sticky, gooey stuff. The result was an unofficial but generally accepted modification to the dress regulations for officers—the adoption of the half-Wellington boot. Most of us purchased them and wore them constantly, often with the bottoms of our trousers tucked into the tops of the boots to keep them out of the mud as we made our way around the airfields. Incidentally, I believe the same situation pertained to the raincoats all officers wore regardless of rank. As far as I know they were never officially approved as "uniform" dress, which is probably why they carried no badges of rank.

Our last flight at OTU was a 3-hour and 35-minute night cross-country which took us to a point about halfway between the Isle of Man and the northwest tip of Wales, thence to the southwest tip of Wales, then inland and north to base again. It is illustrative of the size of the British Isles to note that we completely circumnavigated all of Wales in well under 3 hours flying at less than 200 miles an hour. Altogether at OTU we logged a total of 89 hours and 35 minutes in a period of forty-five days. I graduated with an "above average" assessment as a medium-bomber pilot but I prefer to think that meant we were rated above average as a crew, because crew performance was bound to affect the rating of a pilot.

We were given a short leave before reporting to our next station, 1664 Heavy Conversion Unit, at Dishforth in Yorkshire. We arrived at the HCU on 17 May 1944 for training on four-engine aircraft.

CHAPTER 11

1664 Heavy Conversion Unit 408 (RCAF) Squadron

Probably the most important event at the beginning of our training at 1664 HCU was the assignment to us of a Flight Engineer, W.T. "Wally" Wilkins from Montreal. He was tall, well built, good-looking and pleasant in manner and he, too, had a great sense of humour. He was also unusual in a couple of ways. First, he was a Canadian and secondly, his regimental number was ___A, a pre-war number, not the R___ number of airmen recruited during the war. He had been an aero engine mechanic until he remustered to aircrew.

Up until this time nearly all of the Flight Engineers in Bomber Command had been RAF types, English, Scottish or Welsh. I believe we were the first "all-Canadian" crew, at least on 408 Squadron. The addition of Wally brought our crew up to the standard complement of seven for most RAF and RCAF heavy bombers.

Our first ten days or so at "con unit" were spent on the various phases of familiarization with the Handley Page Halifax Mk V with which it was equipped. These were powered by the Rolls Royce Merlin, the first and only liquid-cooled engine I was to encounter in my wartime flying but about which we had heard only praise. We soon had the impression that neither the aircraft nor the engines were in the best of shape, most having already done service in the front lines of Bomber Command.

Our ground instruction here was designed also to familiarize us with the various systems of the Halifax Mk III with which most 6 Group squadrons were equipped at that time. We learned that some of its systems, particularly the fuel system, could be a pilot's and flight engineer's nightmare. For example, the drill to use the fuel from the six tanks in each wing, all of different capacities, went something like this:

Two tanks one, two tanks three, two tanks five etc, one in each wing. For start-up and take-off, we were told to use tanks 1 and 3 in each wing and use 80 gallons from each, then switch to both tanks 5 with the wing balance cocks open and use 220 gallons. After this we were to switch to tanks 1 and 4 and use 60 gallons at which point tanks 1 were to be shut off and 50 gallons were to be used from each tank 4, again with the wing balance cocks open. Next, tanks 2 and 5 were to be used until the number 5 tanks were empty, at which time tanks 2 and 4 were to be used until tanks 2 were empty. This left enough fuel in tanks 1 and 3 for a little over two hours flying time. The system became even more complicated if overload tanks were fitted in the bomb bay.

Fortunately, by the time we were flying the Halifax on operations, we were given the Mk VII in which the fuel system had been simplified to the point where the flight engineer had merely to turn the main fuel valves on to feed all engines from all tanks. I often wondered how the crews of Hally IIIs coped with its system under trying combat conditions or if the flight engineer became a casualty in flight.

The flying, once begun, was quite intensive. We logged thirty-nine hours and forty-five minutes in the fourteen-day span of the flight program. It began, as usual, with circuits and landings and then went hastily through air-to-air firing, practice bombing, three-engine flying and landings, and fighter affiliation exercises. On the ninth day, or rather night, we were checked out for night flying and three nights later set out on our first night cross-country.

Somewhere in the region of the Mull of Galloway the war-weary starboard inner engine gave up the ghost. I asked Don for a course for base and kept a close eye on the slowly sinking altimeter as the three other equally-tired engines laboured to keep us airborne. We arrived back at Dishforth just as we had descended to circuit height and landed without further problem. We completed our con unit flying during the next two nights with cross-countries of five hours and ten minutes and five hours and thirty minutes' duration. It was without any regret that we bade farewell to the clapped-out Hally Fives.

But there was one memorable moment during that course. We were airborne on a routine combined air-to-air firing and bombing exercise when Howie, the wireless operator, came on the intercom with an urgent, "Hey, listen to this!" Not having much to do on that type of flying he had tuned his receiver to the BBC. What we heard on the intercom was the announcement of the allied invasion of Europe. It was D-Day, 6 June 1944, and we were just one week away from joining a squadron.

Again, we were transported by open truck to our new unit, 408 RCAF (B) Squadron based at RCAF Station Linton-on-Ouse, Yorkshire. Linton was also known as Beaver Base, having in addition two satellite airfields, Tholthorpe and Eastmoor. At Linton were 408 (Goose) and 426 (Thunderbird) Squadrons while Tholthorpe had 420 (Snowy Owl) and 425 (Alouette), and Eastmoor housed 432 (Cougar). The last was also known as the Leaside Squadron, having been adopted by the town of Leaside, Ontario. The truck took us on to the station by a back gate and while progressing along the edge of the field we were able to see some of the aircraft parked on their dispersal sites. Our first reaction was stunned amazement. It sounded something like this:

"What the hell are they?"
"They're Lancs, dummy!"
"Yeah, but look at the engines!"
"They're bloody radials!"
"They look like Hercs!"

In fact, the aircraft were Lancaster Mk IIs with Bristol Hercules VI or XVI engines. Only about 200 had been built, at a time when the British were afraid American entry into the war would cut off the flow of Packard-built Rolls Royce Merlin engines, a fear that was never realized. We had never heard of them and years after the war, when in company with other air force veterans, one was often stared at in disbelief or accused of "line-shooting" if one claimed to have flown operations on Lancasters with radial engines. Those that remained were inherited from the RAF by two or three RCAF squadrons as they approached the end of their useful lives.

We were first assigned quarters, and Don and I drew a room in a house which, pre-war, had been a married senior officer's quarters. All the rooms had been converted to bedrooms and Don and I shared ours with a wireless operator from another crew. We were quite comfortable and I claimed a bed next to the south-facing bay window which held a small table in its shallow "U." The room's greatest advantage was that it was handy to the mess but not in it, as were the quarters of a good many officers.

There were actually two officers' messes, the second in a temporary building some distance away, its members being Pilot Officers. Don and I, having achieved the exalted rank of Flying Officer, were assigned to the principal mess, a fine pre-war building with a comfortable anteroom (as the lounge was known), a games room with a billiard table, dart and shove ha'penny boards, a separate bar and a beautiful dining room with large windows facing east and north.

At each end of the central structure of the building were two-storied living quarters divided into rooms designed for one officer. These now housed at least two with three or four in the larger ones in double-tiered bunks. The mess building formed the base of an isosceles triangle, with the married quarters in which we were housed forming the other two sides.

We arrived at Linton on 15 June and the next day three new pilots and our flight engineers were taken on a familiarization flight during which each pilot occupied the left hand seat for one circuit. Our flight commander, F/L (soon to be S/L) Latimer, was our instructor. We logged twenty minutes dual each. Two days later I flew with a F/L Pullar for an hour and forty-five minutes doing circuits and three-engine landings and the same day did fifty minutes solo with my crew. Our sole preparation for flying the Lanc was a few hours spent with "Pilot's Notes." As we had flown Hercules engines at OTU we were familiar with them but the Lanc was equipped with the Mk VI or XVI of 1650 horsepower.

It took us a while to get used to all the knobs and switches in the array surrounding the pilot and flight engineer while our other crew members also had to familiarize themselves with their new equipment layouts. Even the gun turrets were of a different make and type than those on the Halifax.

On 21 June I got a thirty-minute night checkout and between then and 4 July we did a couple of air-to-air firing exercises combined with two practice bombing sessions and fighter affiliation practices. These were followed by two night cross-countries of 5 hours, 45 minutes and 4 hours, 15 minutes. We then were considered ready for ops with a total of 10 hours and 15 minutes day and 16 hours and 35 minutes night on the Lanc II.

While this was going on our gunners flew some ops with other crews. This was because 408's Lanc IIs had a .50 calibre defensive machine gun on a free mount over a hole in the belly, meaning the crew had to have eight men. To provide the extra man, our gunners were "stolen." My rear gunner, Ralph, flew two ops while Hap, my mid-upper, flew one before the rest of the crew began our tours.

Also during this period, on 23 June, I flew one sortie as "second dickey" with an experienced crew. This was intended to give a novice skipper an idea of what ops were like before he took his own crew out. I flew mine with F/L W.S. Pullar of Calgary, a very experienced pilot. He and two others of his crew were flying their last operation on their second tour, leading Hap and Ralph to offer to bet me even money that I would not return!

Being second pilot on the Lanc II was not a comfortable experience. Naturally, the skipper wanted his flight engineer beside him in the right hand seat so I was relegated to a semi-standing position behind the left hand seat with my backside doing its best not to disturb various implements on the navigator's chart table. About the only cautionary piece of advice I was given was not to clutter up the intercom with needless chatter, in other words, "Keep your trap shut and your eyes open."

The night operation itself was a "piece of cake." Its target was a buzz bomb launching site at Bienque in France. Although from the standpoint of enemy air activity it was uneventful, I did get a good sampling of what both light and heavy flak looked like and I recall distinctly the "twangs," felt more than heard, as our eighteen 500-pound bombs were released one by one, in rapid succession. I felt the upward surge of the aircraft as its load was suddenly lightened by four and a half tons.

On the way back from the target the bomb aimer drew our attention to a blob of flame moving across the countryside far below and ahead of us on the port side. We had heard a good deal about buzz bombs or V-1s but so far had never actually seen one. The speed and direction in which the flame was moving soon convinced us we were watching one and Pullar decided to have a go at it. He stuffed the nose down and rammed the throttles wide open but even diving at close to 300 miles an hour it was soon apparent we would never catch it. The chase was abandoned, much to the disappointment of the bomb aimer who was standing in the nose turret eagerly waiting to fire his two .30 calibre machine guns at it. We completed the trip and landed back at Linton after three hours and fifty minutes in the air, which I entered in my log book with a big black number "1" beside it.

We had one other pre-op misadventure that nearly killed us all. On 29 June we were sent by truck to Eastmoor to pick up a 408 kite that had been left there a day or two before with a minor unserviceability. We started it up and taxied out following instructions from flying control, did our run up and started off.

As we picked up speed and topped a small rise in the runway, I saw a group of men on the runway directly ahead of us. They quickly scurried off to the side. As we got closer to where they had been I suddenly realized that there was a trench on which they had been working which extended halfway across the runway on the right hand side—the side we were on. Flying control had neglected to inform us there was trenching being done across the runway and that we should use the left hand side!

By the time we saw the trench we were going too fast to stop or cut across to the other side. I rammed the throttles wide open and prayed I could jump the aircraft across the ditch which looked to be about three feet wide. The last time I glanced at the airspeed indicator we were doing about seventy miles per hour and in the ensuing couple of hundred yards probably gained another ten or fifteen. As the ditch disappeared under the nose I hauled back on the control column and the aircraft left the ground.

My intention had been to jump the ditch and finish the take-off run normally on the other side but, to my surprise, the aircraft stayed airborne. Without bombs and with a small fuel load the bellowing Hercs, cranking out their full 1650 horsepower each, kept us in the air but in a decidedly unflyable attitude, nose high and tail almost dragging. We must have flown at least four or five miles before I was able to coax the plane into a normal flying attitude at a decent airspeed. Fortunately, there were no high obstacles off the end of the runway.

After landing at Linton, I informed my flight commander of Eastmoor flying control's dereliction of duty but I heard no more about the incident. I can only hope someone got his or her knuckles severely rapped. It came within a hairsbreadth of costing the RCAF one Lancaster and seven men, but it increased my respect for the Lancaster immeasurably.

Our first sortie as a crew took place in daylight on 6 July and the target was another buzz bomb site. This one was at Coquereux in northwestern France to which we carted the usual eighteen 500-pound bombs. This was a "three point op." By this time the RCAF had changed its method of setting the length of an operational tour to a point system. The number of points awarded for each trip was based on the degree of opposition encountered, the length of the trip and so on. Thus, most targets in northwest France were three pointers and most German targets were four pointers, while a hundred and twenty points or thereabouts comprised a complete tour.

On 7 July we had a much more interesting trip when we were sent out in daylight again with a load of eleven 1000-pounders and four 500-pounders to bomb a concentration of German tanks, guns and armour near Caen in front of the Canadian Army. We apparently achieved good results because we were sent a congratulatory message from the army which was read to us at our next briefing. But this trip added another to our list of adventures.

We were among the last back and while still an hour or so from base could hear on the R/T that the circuit was stacked up with many aircraft pleading shortages of fuel. As we, too, were getting low on fuel I decided not to return to base but to land and refuel somewhere short of Linton. To this end, I called the "Darky Watch," the Bomber Command emergency system, and asked for a landing spot. I immediately got a response, explained my predicament, and as it was getting dark asked the airfield to turn on its runway lights. Three sets of runway lights came on! I solved the identification problem by asking the one I was talking to on the radio to fire a rocket which they did. We landed and found we were on an RAF Wellington OTU less than an hour's flying time from Linton.

By this time it was dark and the OTU had packed up operations for the day. However, they called out an engineering officer who said he would arrange the refuelling and suggested we go to the airmen's mess for a bite to eat while he got his crew rounded up and into action. We accepted and were taken to the filthiest eating establishment I have ever encountered, before or since. We confined our meal to toast made in a coal-or coke-fired heating stove, with margarine and some type of jam. This we ate at a filthy table still covered with the remnants of the last meal which included a couple of scraps of uneaten bread. As we sat there, Howie suddenly exclaimed, "It moved!" and pointed to a piece of bread on the table. We all watched and sure enough, it moved again. We flipped it over with a knife exposing three or four giant cockroaches that scurried around the table top looking for cover. We left.

On returning to the aircraft we found no activity but were told our kite had been refuelled. We got on board and were getting ready to start up when Wally swore loudly and exclaimed, "Look! The stupid bastards have put it all in one tank!" In fact, they had put all of the 400 gallons we had requested in the port inboard 580-gallon tank. As a result we sat for about an hour with a trolley-ack plugged in while

Wally used our internal pumps to redistribute the fuel and make it accessible to all four engines.

This done we were about to taxi out for take-off when flying control asked if we were sure their runway was long enough for us. In effect, we said, "Just watch us!" We did our run up, turned onto the runway and locked the brakes while we ran the engines up to full bore. I released the brakes and we leaped forward. When we passed the control tower at the midpoint of the runway we were a hundred feet in the air.

We had one more surprise awaiting us. When we got back to Linton we found everything had been closed down. There was no one available to debrief us and we discovered that our aircraft had been struck off as "pranged." I learned later that Linton had heard our call to the "Darky Watch" but as we descended to land, our transmission suddenly cut off so they assumed we had "gone in." Why the OTU had not messaged them that we had landed there, as they were supposed to do, we don't know, but judging from what we had seen of the station, we weren't surprised.

Our next flight was an air-to-air firing exercise and practice bombing but on 15 July we were off again at night to a buzz bomb launching site at Bois des Jardins, carrying eleven 1000-pounders and four 500-pounders. Results were good, as one of the bombs exploded a buzz bomb on the launching ramp which was so thoroughly destroyed it was never used again.

After this trip we were granted nine days' leave under the system then in use by 6 Group. In this scheme we were on duty for six weeks, seven days a week, after which we were given the equivalent of seven "Sundays" plus a 48-hour pass, making a total of nine days. I made it a custom to take leave with one or more members of the crew. As all were NCOs except Don this caused some problems in finding accommodation as the various military clubs run by the Brits mostly were for officers or for other ranks. We surmounted this problem by staying in commercial hotels or privately operated accommodation.

On one of our early leaves in Edinburgh, Hap Sharpe and I were directed to a private home that took in servicemen on leave, providing room only. It was operated by a very talkative Scottish lady with an extremely rich accent and a decided prejudice against the "Sassenach," as she termed the English. After we had checked in and dropped our kit we began to leave but she stopped us in the foyer for a lecture on conduct while on leave. It went something like this:

> "I ken ye sodjer laddies. Ye're gaein' after the gir-r-r-ls. But y'ken, this toon is full o' Sassenach refugees. Stay away frae them. Find yersels some nice Scottish lassies. Why, just last week my wee Scotty dog went oot and took up wi' some English slut. He got distemper an' we had t' hae him put to sleep!"

That was the only time in my entire life I have heard of a bitch being termed a "slut."

As we departed we encountered a problem. We lit cigarettes and discovered we had used our last match, an item which was not always easy to find in wartime Britain. We solved the problem temporarily by smoking alternately, each lighting a cigarette from the butt of the other's last before it was discarded. Downtown, we explored several tobacco shops before finding one with a limited supply of wooden matches they were saving for their regulars but who took pity on us and sold us a small box each.

While we were absent from Linton new aircraft—Halifax Mk VIIs—had begun to arrive and although we continued to fly operations on the Lancs we spent a couple of days flying circuits, practise bombing, doing fighter affiliation and air tests on the Halifaxes. My conversion this time comprised two dual circuits and one solo circuit in daylight. After having flown the Lancaster, we pilots were not too impressed by the Halifax which, in contrast, was like driving a ten-ton truck without power steering after being used to a fine sedan.

Our next op on the Lanc was one of the "big" ones, the dock and industrial areas of Hamburg at night. Our bomb load consisted of one 4000 pound high capacity bomb (thin skinned and mostly explosive) and sixteen 500-pounders. With the fuel for well over six hours' flying and the bomb load, it was by far my heaviest load for take-off so far, but as we used to say affectionately of the Lanc II, it "would lift anything that was loose." Needless to say, I experienced no difficulty with the take-off.

But the Lanc II had one feature which we disliked intensely—its Rotol electric propellers. We were warned they had been known to run away—that is, when taking off in full fine pitch the prop blades occasionally would go past the full fine position so they were flat to the plane of their rotation, producing no thrust and causing the engine to overspeed and sometimes to depart from the aircraft. As a result, when taking off the flight engineer's fingers hovered always over the "increase/decrease pitch" switches, ready to check instantly any tendency for the propellers to exceed maximum take-off rpms.

Our trip to and from Hamburg was relatively uneventful but we certainly encountered more flak than we had dreamed possible. Because of our use of Window (thousands of radar-jamming aluminum foil strips) the flak was barrage type, not radar-predicted, so the chances of being hit we figured at about one in 200. We saw no enemy fighters nor did we witness any fighter engagements with other aircraft so it was with a great sense of disbelief and shock that we learned four aircraft from our squadron had failed to return, including our flight commander, S/L G.B. Latimer who earlier had given me my first checkout on the Lanc. All of the four crews we lost had done more than twenty operational flights each.

One of Latimer's crew members was Lieutenant A.A. Hauzenberger of the US Army Air Force, an American who had joined the RCAF before the US entered the war. As did many others, he had transferred to the USAAF but had elected to finish his stint with his Canadian crew. He stood out in his American khaki and "pinks" uniform and, most remarkably, when he flew he was a veritable walking arsenal. In addition to his Canadian-issue .38 Smith and Wesson revolver he carried the standard US issue .45 automatic, a smaller automatic pistol and a very impressive hunting knife in a sheath at his waist. The reason was that he was Jewish and swore the Nazis would never take him alive. I never learned what happened to him.

The loneliness characteristic of night raids soon impressed itself on us. Usually there were several hundred aircraft in the bomber stream but one could fly an entire operation without seeing another one, and while one crew might describe a trip as fraught with danger from enemy aircraft and flak, another might find it the proverbial piece of cake.

This trip introduced us to the use of Window, the code name for the aluminum foil strips that our wireless operator shoved down the window chute at specified intervals. Their purpose was to jam enemy fighter control radars as the reflections cast by the strips almost completely covered the enemy's radar screens with a myriad of returns, each representing an aircraft, while the reflections from actual aircraft were lost in cover. The bundles of aluminum strips were supposed to be tossed out at specified intervals but Howie, completely convinced of their efficacy, used to scrounge as many more bundles as he could get over each aircraft's allotment, and toss them out at the correct intervals and in between as well!

Another countermeasure we had went under the code name Tinsel. When not otherwise involved, our wireless ops swept the VHF radio band listening for German fighter directors giving intercept instructions to their fighters. When one was heard the wireless op backtuned his VHF transmitter to the same frequency and and held down his morse key. This resulted in the noise from our starboard inner engine being picked up by a microphone in the nacelle and broadcast on the German controller's frequency. Howie claimed to have heard controllers screaming in frustration at the inability of fighters to understand their orders.

Our sixth sortie was an abortive one. On 1 August we carried eighteen 500-pound bombs toward a buzz bomb site at Ferme de Forestelle only to be called off by the master bomber when we were six minutes from the target. The area was so heavily covered by cloud it was impossible to see the target markers or the tiny target so we carried our bombs home again. However, we were credited with a three-point op anyway.

My flight engineer deserved the credit for the success of our seventh op. When we ran up our engines prior to taxiing out for take-off, we had a terrific mag drop on the port inner engine. When running up our engines the rpms were watched as each of the two magnetos on each engine was switched off. If there was more than about a 50-rpm drop with one magneto off, the engine was considered to be unserviceable. In this case we had a drop of more than 150 rpm.

As soon as we had shut the engines down, Wally went out the upper escape hatch onto the port wing, stretched out on the nacelle so he could reach over the cowling and began feeling each of the fourteen hot cylinders with his bare hands. He soon detected one that was cooler than the rest and hollered for the groundcrew to bring a maintenance stand and a couple of new spark plugs. This was done, the cowling was removed, the plugs changed on the cool cylinder, the cowling replaced and we fired the engine up again. This time all checked out and we proceeded to take off—almost an hour late. Now it was time for Don to do his stuff.

Tactics for this daylight raid were for 6 Group to fly south over England to rendezvous with aircraft from other groups over Reading at set time intervals, from which point course was to be set for the target with all the aircraft grouped into a "bomber stream."

Don gave me a course which took us on a shortcut diagonally southeast to the point where the bomber stream was to cross the French coast and we caught up with them there. We bombed the target on time, unloading seven 1000-pounders and four 500-pound bombs. The target was Bois de Cassan, a storage site for buzz bombs and later photo recce found we had damaged or destroyed fifty-six storage bunkers, railroad tracks, roads, and had damaged other buildings as well as some flak towers.

Our next trip was our last in the Lanc II. It was a daylight op to St. Leu d'Esserent, another buzz bomb site. What we didn't know and were never told was that the Jerries were storing buzz bombs in giant limestone caves which Frenchmen had used for growing mushrooms. Our eleven 1000-pound and four 500-pound bombs, like those of the other aircraft on the raid, were mostly ineffective against the caves but the servicing railroads were damaged. I learned long after the war that later the caves were successfully attacked by Lancasters using the Tallboy bomb, a six-ton medium capacity bomb carried by specially modified Lancasters of 100 Group, descendants of the famed "Dambusters." These effectively put the buzz-bomb-storage caves out of operation and caused a notable decrease in the number launched against Britain for a significant period of time.

Although our remaining Lancs still were serviceable we never flew them on ops again. We made a few flights in them—air tests and ferry flights to an RAF Conversion Unit—but all of our future sorties were to be done on the Hally VII. We were not happy with the change but there was nothing we could do about it. And we would have to give up singing our 408 "theme song," sung to the tune of an English military ditty, "Bless Them All," dating back to the days of the British Raj and military service in India:

> "They say there's a Lancaster leaving the Ruhr,
> Bound for old Blighty shore,
> Heavily laden with terrified men,
> Shit scared and prone on the floor.
> There's many a Junkers that's hot on their tail,
> Many a Messerschmitt too. They've shot off our bollocks
> and fucked our hydraulics
> So cheer up my lads, bless them all!"

CHAPTER 12
Halifax VII

Summer 1944

> Ops in a Hally,
> Ops in a Hally,
> Who'll go on ops
> in a Hally with me?
> And he sang as he sat
> and waited while his engines warmed,
> Who'll go on ops in a Hally with me?
> (sung to the tune of "Waltzing Mathilda")

There were many features about the Halifax Mk VII we didn't like. For me, the throttle quadrant was a bit of a problem. The throttle controls were four straight half-inch diameter rods projecting about eight or ten inches above the throttle quadrant and just far enough apart that with my somewhat smaller than average hands I could barely span all four. I had some difficulty in handling them differentially. In contrast, the throttles on the Lancaster were arranged so those for the outboard engines were bent inward at almost a right angle over those for the inboard engines, making a very convenient and easy to handle cluster, especially convenient for taxiing as steering on the ground was done by differential use of throttle on the outboard engines.

One particularly strange characteristic of the Hally as compared to the Lanc II was that although they both had basically the same Hercules engines the torque effect on the Hally was much stronger, giving it a decided tendency to swing to starboard on take-off if the throttles were opened carelessly and too quickly. To overcome this problem one had to open the throttles differentially with the starboard outer leading the others and the starboard inner a little ahead of the port engines until enough speed had been gained to have rudder control. Again, with my small hands this was a bit of a problem. On the Lanc II the four throttles could be advanced almost in parallel with little evidence of torque attempting to swing the aircraft.

Another big difference between the two was the landing characteristics. The Lanc had a tendency to "float." We used to say you could round out the Lanc a few feet above the ground, cut the throttles and light a cigarette while you waited for it to touch down smoothly on the runway. The Halifax fell onto the ground. If you rounded out ten feet up and cut the throttles, the aircraft dropped like a load of bricks.

I was rarely able to make smooth landings in the Halifax. My rear gunner and I used to joke about this. He would claim he should finish his tour first because on take-off he was always airborne some time before the rest of us, while I countered that with my landings, occasionally touching down tail wheel first, he was first on the ground!

A plus feature of the Halifax was the flight engineer's station. His engine instruments, temperature gauges, fuel gauges and so on were mounted on a panel facing forward in a space behind the pilot which gave the flight engineer room to work and removed some of the clutter from the pilot's instrument panel. One disadvantage was that the pilot couldn't see the fuel gauges except by twisting his neck almost 180 degrees. Another nice feature of the Hally was that its fuselage was much roomier than that of the Lanc.

Getting in and out of the Lanc was always a struggle as the pilot, navigator, bomb aimer, wireless op and flight engineer had to drag their gear and parachutes over the wing spars with little overhead clearance. The Halifax fuselage allowed one to stand up and, between the two wing spars which traversed the fuselage, was the "centre rest position" with two padded benches along the fuselage walls. These could be used as bunks if any of the crew were wounded. During take-off and landing they were the normal position for all of the crew except the pilot, flight engineer and tail gunner, being the area of the aircraft least susceptible to damage in event of a prang.

Our next operational flight at night on 7 August was nearly our last. We flew it in Halifax NP713 which was a clunker in more ways than one, as we were to learn to our sorrow. It was obvious the maintenance on the base from which it had come to us was not up to 6 Group's standards.

The target was German troop and armour concentrations near Caen in Normandy not far inland from the invasion beaches. We were to bomb so close to our own troops that we were told unless we could identify the target positively we were not to bomb and were to bring our bombs back to prove we hadn't. We brought ours back.

On return we joined the aircraft stacked up over Linton waiting their turn to land. Our turn came to join the circuit and on the downwind leg we selected wheels down. As they locked into position their green lights on the instrument panel came on blindingly. I told Wally to switch the cover to "night" but when he tried to do so he found it was stuck and wouldn't turn to the shielded night position.

Not wanting to lose our turn to land I called the tower and told them we were going to extend our downwind leg a bit and would tell them when we had the problem fixed. The tower OK'd this. Wally was chewing gum so I told him to stick his gum over the glaring lights. He did, I turned a 180, lined up with the runway, called "Funnel" to the Linton tower and got the "Pancake"; that is, permission to land.

We made a normal landing and coasted down the runway for about half its length. I began to apply the brakes and the aircraft slowed slightly but the brakes faded rapidly and in only a moment were completely ineffective. I knew we wouldn't be able to make the turn onto the taxiway at the end of the runway but wasn't unduly concerned as I knew there was a long clear overshoot area off the end of Linton's main north-south runway which we were using.

Suddenly there was a nerve-shattering crash and the aircraft ground to a halt on its belly, the propellers stopping with a clatter after digging up several yards of potatoes. My head snapped forward as the Sutton harness restrained my body and for a moment I sat unbelieving, dazed and confused before the sound of gasoline pouring from the ruptured wing tanks brought me to my senses and I flicked off the engine switches on my instrument panel.

I called into the intercom something like, "Get out!" and as I undid my harness saw Wally streaking aft past me from the bomb aimer's position in the nose to which he had been precipitated by the impact. I made my way out and checked that we were all safely clear of the aircraft but couldn't find Howie. I shouted his name and he replied—from the other side of three rolls of barbed concertina wire which somehow he had run right over without even tearing his clothes! All of the crew was safely out.

We soon discovered the reason for our prang. We had landed at Eastmoor, not Linton! The north ends of their two runways were only six miles apart and when I stretched the downwind leg, and made the 180-degree turn we had drifted eastward enough so that the runway I saw in front of me was the wrong one. I had touched down between two of Eastmoor's aircraft with one still on the runway ahead of us and another touching down just behind us. At least we were out of the way of the second in a hurry!

I remember practically nothing of that night after we were all clear of the aircraft but we were bedded down at Eastmoor and in the morning were taken out to survey the damage and collect our gear. We were surprised to discover we were not the only ones in the same potato patch. Two of Eastmoor's kites which had landed ahead of us had done the same thing. One had veered slightly to the left, the other to the right and we had gone in between them so the three pranged aircraft were in an almost perfect "Vic" formation. It was very lucky that none of the three had caught fire as among us we were still carrying sixteen and a half tons of bombs.

Our aircraft was a write-off, its back broken just ahead of the main spar, the undercart ripped off with pieces sticking up through huge holes in the wings and flaps, cowlings full of dirt and all four propellers bent into grotesque shapes. And the pillagers had been at it already. The clocks and other desirable bits were gone from the instrument panels and some of our personal gear had been "won" by someone.

The thing that annoyed me most was that the buckshee Irving jacket Howie had somehow got was gone—this because Howie had promised me that after we finished our tour, if we finished a tour, he would give it to me. Those jackets, leather and sheepskin lined, were a much coveted item once issued to RAF fighter pilots.

The aftermath of this was a red endorsement in my logbook, signed by Johnny Fauquier, stating I had overshot on touchdown and consequently couldn't stop, which was not what had happened. As for the subsequent Board of Inquiry, I was not called to testify as to what had happened. But what really got to me was an interview with the squadron OC a day or two after the prang.

He asked me what had happened and after I had told him, he said I shouldn't worry about it as he had flown the same aircraft checking out a new pilot the day before and the brakes were so bad he had to taxi on the grass to keep the aircraft slowed down! Why he hadn't put the aircraft unserviceable I'll never know. The only possible reason I can think of is that at the time, 6 Group HQ was calling for maximum efforts, with the squadrons putting every available kite into the air.

The only physical result of the prang for me was a very sore and stiff neck which persisted, slowly diminishing in intensity for several years until about nine years later. In 1953 I was doing landscaping around a new house my wife and I were renting in Ottawa when I suddenly developed such an acute pain in my neck I couldn't move. Subsequent X-rays revealed bits were missing from two vertebrae in my neck and the disc between them had been crushed. Since then I always have had some degree of pain in my neck which time has taught me to ignore unless it is aggravated by some thoughtless action.

On August 14 we flew a daylight army cooperation raid in the Caen-Falaise area which went astray terribly with disastrous results for our soldiers on the ground. Somehow bombs were dropped short of the target area. I have never learned the precise cause but it was speculated that a Pathfinder aircraft had been shot down, crashing just short of the target area and that its target markers had exploded, deceiving the early bomb aimers into dropping their bombs too soon. By the time we got to the target area there was so much dust and smoke Johnny couldn't identify the aiming point so we brought our bombs back again—this time with much happier results on landing!

Early in August someone decided that if we were to continue to do ops in daylight, perhaps we should be able to fly in formation for mutual defence. A token effort was made to practice formation flying, as on 6 August when we spent an hour and forty minutes in company with two other kites flying in formation locally. In the event, we never did fly formation on daylight ops although we did once over the English Channel on the homeward flight from a target in France.

In the period from 1 August to 15 August we flew nine sorties, six in daylight and three at night including the disastrous one just described. Three of these were memorable for various reasons. On the night of 10 August we attacked U-boat refueling installations at La Pallice with sixteen 500-pound bombs. The striking thing about this op was the fantastic display of flak we encountered.

As we approached the target the sky ahead was literally filled with the stuff. It looked like an American Fourth of July fireworks celebration, with tracer of various colours streaking in every direction, arcing over and then disappearing. It seemed nothing could fly through it. As we got closer we realized with relief most of it was light flak that couldn't reach our altitude.

It was also on this op we had our first and only experience of being "coned" by searchlights. Happily, they were British. Our return track took us over Southampton and apparently we arrived there just as a German tip-and-run raid was in progress. We could see some flak activity as we approached but, as at La Pallice, it was all light stuff and far below us. However we must have been detected by a searchlight battery's radar as suddenly a half dozen searchlights locked on to us. It showed us just how blinding and panic-making it could be.

As I waited for Howie to give me the recognition letters for the time period I'm sure I hunched my shoulders in anticipation of a cluster of heavy flak shells bursting around us. Howie gave me the letters and I flashed them on our downward identification light, wondering at the same time if the gunners could see our pitifully small ident light in the reflected glare of their own brilliant lights. Either they did or someone in the battery was good at aircraft recognition because the lights just as suddenly snapped off. We heaved great sighs of relief and proceeded on our way.

It was on the return from a daylight raid in this period that our flight rendezvous'd to fly home in formation. A new flight commander who was universally disliked was to lead the formation. We formed in Vics of three with the flight commander leading the first while I led the second below and behind his. R/T discipline went to hell in a handbasket as several pilots, revelling in the anonymity of radio, took the opportunity to tell the flight commander what they thought of him in very unflattering terms. I gave him a blast as well but for good reason.

He was using Very pistol flares to govern the formation and one he fired arced upward and came down to bounce off our port wing between the two engines. With the thought in mind of what could have happened if it had been sucked into an oil cooler on top of one of the engines, I offered him some pointed advice on what he could do with his Very pistol and to pull the trigger when he got it there.

Another raid around this time did our hearts good. We went in daylight to pound a German night fighter drome at Melsbroek near Brussels. We carried nine 1000-pounders and four 500s and there was considerable damage done to runways, buildings and central dispersal sites. Revenge was sweet after the losses our squadron had taken at their hands. We sincerely hoped we had caught them all in bed.

Kiel, 16 August 1944. This one stands out in my memory as we only survived because of what we termed "horse-shit luck." We were carrying one 2000-pounder plus incendiaries and the trip out was not unusual. But the flak over the target area was intense, some of it close enough for us to hear the shells exploding, and there definitely were night fighters operating. In fact, we came close to colliding with one.

As we ran up to the aiming point Wally suddenly clutched for the microphone switch on his oxygen mask and raised his other arm to point. He quickly got his mike on but just said, "Never mind, it's gone." I had looked up as he raised his arm and heard, rather than saw, another aircraft roar past just over our heads, flying at nearly 180 degrees to us. Wally got a glimpse of it and said it was a Junkers 88. I doubt if the Jerry saw us but if he did it wasn't in time for him to bring his guns to bear.

We were on the bomb run when the starboard outer engine suddenly quit cold with no warning whatsoever. Wally determined which engine it was by checking the rpms on prop pitch change and hit the propeller feathering button while I struggled to hold the aircraft straight for Johnny's bomb run. Instead of the prop feathering, the circuit's fuses blew.

After what seemed like ages, Johnny gave me the "Bombs gone," Howie changed the fuses in the feathering circuit and we tried again. This time, everything electrical in the aircraft went U/S except the engine instruments.

With the starboard outer propeller windmilling, rudder trim couldn't make up for all the drag and I had to brace both of my feet on the left rudder pedal to hold the aircraft straight. We headed out for England over the North Sea. As we had no radios operating I asked Don to give me a course for Carnaby, an emergency drome on Flamborough Head and the nearest runway in England to northern Germany. This he did and navigated the rest of the way with Johnny holding a flashlight over his chart table. It was common scuttlebutt that the sea off Flamborough Head was full of aircraft that didn't quite make it.

As we struggled along the fuselage suddenly filled with smoke and Wally said it was coming from the JB6, the main electrical junction box on the starboard side of the fuselage. Howie dashed up from his position and after he and Wally had undone a few of the wing nuts securing the cover, Howie ripped the cover off the remaining nuts and smothered the smouldering insulation on the wires inside with his gloved hands. I am sure that under normal circumstances he wouldn't have been able even to bend that cover, let alone rip it out from under several wing nuts.

Shortly after, Hap in the mid-upper turret said he thought he could see sparks coming from the starboard outer but he wasn't sure whether they were actually from that engine or from the outboard exhaust of the starboard inner. I decided that since the outer had been dead for an hour, they must be from the inner which we were working a little harder than usual.

Every once in a while Don would come on the intercom to inform me gently that I was drifting off course to starboard. I was grateful for Howie's assistance on the left rudder pedal by pulling on it from his position below and in front of me. Suddenly a terrific explosion somewhere out in the starboard wing shook the whole airframe. No one could see any evidence of resulting damage nor was there any indication that anything else was wrong beyond what we already had encountered. We flew on.

Thanks to Don's accurate navigation and Howie's assistance in keeping us on course, the first light we saw in England was the flashing occult at Carnaby. We had no radios working so as we approached the runway Wally fired the Very pistol loaded with the colours of the day and we got a flashing green light from the control tower. I'm sure we all breathed sighs of relief as the undercarriage came down and locked into position. We went straight in and landed without any further problem. We followed a Carnaby vehicle to a parking spot and shut down the three operating engines.

I was so exhausted, both physically and emotionally, I remember nothing more of the night—where we slept or if we slept, where we were fed or if we were fed—but I remember the next morning very distinctly for a number of reasons. First, we were taken to a flight room where we were to await being picked up by a Linton kite. There were two other crews waiting as well, one Canadian and a Free French crew from 4 Group.

The Canadians had been the victims in the target area of a brush with another Halifax that had swept over them, taking the pilot's canopy off with one of its propellers. The pilot sat in the flight room with us and his crew, the front of his battledress jacket caked with dried blood from the cuts on his face, severely lacerated by broken shards of the canopy. Flying that aircraft back to Carnaby must have been a terrible ordeal.

Forty-nine years later, after I had written a short account of this adventure for a 408 Squadron veterans' newsletter, I was telephoned at my home in Winnipeg by this pilot from Ontario. It gave me a feeling of great joy to learn he had survived the war. He certainly deserved it.

The Free French crew had a much different adventure. When they dropped their bombs an incendiary cluster bomb had hung up and they were unable to get rid of it. Each of these bombs consisted of ninety 4-pound incendiaries strapped around an explosive charge that would disperse them.

The risky part for the Frenchmen was that these bombs were barometrically fused, that is set to explode at a certain altitude after being released. If the nature of their hang-up had been such that the arming wire on the bomb had been pulled free and the bomb had armed itself, they could expect to have been blown to eternity when they let down to land. The nervous anticipation as they descended through the critical altitude must have been heart stopping. I have often wondered if I would even have tried to land it—the nylon safety promised by a parachute would have had an almost irresistible appeal in those circumstances.

While we were waiting a ground crew man came in and asked who had been flying Halifax NP713. I told him I had and he asked if I would like to have a look at it. I went with him down a long line of damaged aircraft to ours which had a maintenance stand set up at the starboard outer, with the upper nacelle covers behind the engine removed. Looking into the nacelle I was shocked beyond belief.

All of the wiring behind the fire wall had been melted into unidentifiable blobs, the main petrol line to the engine was burned through, the main wing spar had been burnt part way through and there were blisters in the self-sealing covering of the wing petrol tanks the size of grapefruit halves.

The airman reached down into the nacelle and handed me a piece of bright shiny copper. It was a piece of the engine's fire extinguisher cylinder. If, when Hap had reported sparks coming from the engine Wally and I had pressed the fire extinguisher button, the cylinder would have discharged its contents uselessly on the engine in front of the firewall. As it was, the inside of the nacelle had become so hot the fire extinguisher exploded and put the fire out—which accounted for the explosion we had heard out over the North Sea. There was nothing obviously visible to explain the cause of the fire. Perhaps a small splinter of flak had shorted the wiring in the nacelle.

On such bits of fortuitous luck do the lives of men depend in wartime. My crew members termed it "horse shit luck" and I agreed wholeheartedly.

We filled in a couple of days after this doing training exercises, practice bombing, fighter affiliation and a two and a half hour cross-country so Don could practice using the H2S ground-searching radar with which the Hally VII was equipped. By this time it was known, however, that the Germans had equipped their night fighters with a homing device which could lock on to our H2S transmissions from forty miles away, so its use over enemy territory was severely restricted.

Our intelligence had learned also that our tail-searching radar known as Monica, intended to warn us of the approach of enemy fighters from the rear, could be used by the Jerries to track us from as far away as fifty miles, so its use was discontinued.

One fighter affiliation exercise ended in an amusing incident. This one was done with a Spitfire. It was usual for us after such an exercise to lead the fighter to a known spot so he could find his way back to his own base. This Spitfire we led to Linton with him flying formation on our starboard wing. As we joined the circuit, I waved goodbye to him but he didn't depart. In fact, when we were almost on the runway, he was still in formation on our wing tip! However, as soon as we were about to touch down he opened his throttle and streaked ahead of us and away doing a vertical roll as he departed.

There were other light moments as well. Three of us who enjoyed singing often got together in the bar of the mess on quiet evenings and sang, mostly barber shop style. There was an RCAF Womens' Division officer who used to enjoy our efforts so it became the custom for us to perch her in a corner on one of the high bar stools and serenade her. I only hope her enjoyment of this was honest! The other two pilots involved were "Muzz" Faulder and Bob Clothier; the latter, incidentally, flew 408 squadron's 3000th sortie during his second tour of ops. I believe it was Clothier, too, who was mainly responsible for the lyrics we sang to the tune of "My Heart Belongs to Daddy." They went like this:

We're four-oh-eight
We've got a date
To meet the Hun in open battle,
At fifteen thou' above the cloud
You can hear that ack-ack rattle.

It's the Ruhr tonight
With searchlights bright
And Focke Wulfs to add their deadly prattle
But we'll have our fun despite the Hun
And we'll mow them down like cattle.

Oh, we'll drop our bombs on Essen,
Leave those fires burning so swell.
Yes, wc'll drop our bombs on Essen
And Hitler loves us-like hell!
(Repeat last four lines)

And now we're back
And dead on track
To streak down that last silvery mile.
We've had our fun despite the Hun-
Give us a Waf and a pint of mild!

After the female officers had gone, the lyrics of some of our songs became a little more ribald as, for example, our version of "Colonel Bogey," to which we sang our derisive description of the Nazi leadership. It went like this:

Hitler has only got one ball.
Goering has two but they are small,
Himmler, is somewhat sim'lar
But Doctor Goe-bals has no balls at all.

Another amusing incident in that bar concerned a Wing Commander Smith, 6 Group's Engineering Officer, who visited the station occasionally. He was physically a giant of a man, all muscle, who filled the entire front seat of the little Hillman staff car he drove. I was standing one night shoulder to shoulder with several others so we occupied the entire length of the bar. Smith came in and wishing to get to the bar, spanned my buttocks with his right hand, lifted me up, turned and put me down—all with one hand. At the time I weighed about 125 pounds.

German gun emplacements at Point Robert near Brest were the target on the night of 25 August for our next load of nine 1000-pound and four 500-pound bombs. This raid was in aid of the army which was advancing up the French coast. On return, Linton was weathered in so we were diverted to a station at Westcott, south of London, returning to Linton the next day.

In daylight on 27 August, we carried two 1000-pound and thirteen 500-pounders to what we were told was a buzz bomb site at Mimoyeques, near Calais. I learned long after the war that not only did we not know just what we were bombing, neither did Allied intelligence! They knew only that some mysterious and huge construction project involving large excavations and vast quantities of concrete was being worked on by the Germans.

They found out when the site was overrun by the army that the Jerries were building about fifty 6-inch underground "gun" barrels, 416 feet long, aimed at London. They were intended to fire projectiles, speeded up by extra charges exploded behind them as they went up the barrel. However, the Germans never were able to overcome some of the technical problems involving the stability of the projectiles before time ran out for them. The German code name for the effort was *HochDruckPumpe* (High Pressure Pump) and had they got it to work, it certainly would have put the pressure on London as it was designed to fire ten 300-pound projectiles a minute. I can only hope that our raid delayed the project until our army captured the site.

On 31 August we gave the army a hand again by bombing gun emplacements on the Ile de Cezembre at the entrance to St. Malo harbour in daylight. We carried nine 1000-pounders and four 500-hundreds on an op that was unusual in several ways. First, the island was much longer than it was wide but barely long enough for a whole stick of bombs to land on it. Second, the weather was terrible with rain and low cloud. Third, the island was so narrow that we almost had to queue up and take turns to bomb it. In fact, we and another Halifax started the bomb run with another Halifax side by side and I think we were the first on the target. In the event, neither I nor the other pilot wanted to give way and we wound up crowding each other off and had to go around and make a second run.

We finally bombed from 1400 feet while some, who attacked even lower, brought back pieces of their own bombs. The target was so small that on our go around we saw several sticks go down with the first of each going into the sea, bombs two to twelve marching the length of the island and the last going into the sea at the other end. When we made our run Johnny gave me the usual corrections, said "Bombs gone!" and the next thing I heard over the intercom was the chatter of his single Vickers machine gun as he sprayed the island with bullets. Ralph, in the tail turret, gave it a few hundred rounds from his four Brownings as well.

The British press reported that the island was surrendered the next day by its commander who couldn't stop weeping. It was not much wonder as we had put eleven squadrons on a target not much bigger than a race track, adding up to something over 700 tons of high explosive and steel.

August had been a record month for 6 Group. We flew 3700 sorties, more than any other Group in Bomber Command and with

13,000 tons of bombs dropped, exceeded those dropped by the Group in all of 1943 by 400 tons. It was also during late August, on the 28th and 29th, that we ferried two Lanc IIs to an RAF training unit at Bottesford in East Anglia along with two other crews on similar missions. On the 28th we were picked up and returned to Linton by another Lancaster that was more than somewhat crowded with four five-man crews aboard! On the 29th we went alone and returned to York by rail which led to a very unpleasant incident.

We lugged our gear, parachutes and Mae Wests, nav and wireless bags, to the station's deserted and dark taxi rank and went in search of something to eat. We managed to find some sausage rolls and returned to discover a group of RAF aircrew NCOs from 4 Group to the south had moved our stuff back and taken first place in the queue. We immediately leap-frogged our things to their original position and took up station again ahead of them.

One, a sergeant pilot, took loud vocal exception to our action by declaring if I weren't wearing a flat hat he'd knock my block off. I took my officer's forage cap off, tossed it to Hap, and said something like, "OK, it's dark here and I have no cap on so what are you going to do about it?"

He soon showed me but made a big mistake in execution. He took a wild swing at my face with bags of follow-through. I side-stepped it and his follow-through carried him right past me to where he encountered Wally's closed fist going the other way. We were near the outside edge of the sidewalk and I am sure his feet never touched the ground before he hit the wall of the station. It was a beautiful punch. Just at that moment a taxi pulled up, we piled ourselves and our gear into it and left for Linton while the obstreperous one's companions were busy tending their dazed friend.

Late in August after several weeks of hectic operations Group HQ ordered a stand down. Both of our squadrons, air and ground crews, were summoned by the CO to one of the hangars and told to bring something to drink from. When we were assembled a tractor came in towing a string of bomb trolleys loaded with barrels of beer. They were big wooden barrels, each at least forty or fifty gallons capacity. The beer had been well shaken up by its ride on the trolley, was warmish, and turned out to be more lively than British wartime draught beer usually was.

Leaning over the first barrel the CO knocked the bung out and a stream of beer jetted toward the roof of the hangar taking his gold-braided cap with it! The beer lasted for an hour or so with some crews carting it off to corners in buckets into which they dipped everything from NAAFI mugs to tin cans. One enterprising individual had come equipped with a large porcelain chamber pot with which he squatted contentedly on the concrete floor, thus having to make very few trips to the barrels.

One strange but welcome effect was produced by this get-together. As a rule, crews were highly insular and it was very infrequent that any group of entire crews got together. This isolation was increased even further by the fact that some of us were officers while the rest were Warrant Officers or NCOs. As a result some of us, including me, knew few members of the other crews on the squadron very well. However, there was another pilot I got to know quite well. His name was Smith and he had been a teacher of biology at one of the universities in California. A Canadian, he left the US to join the air force. Sadly, he didn't live long after I got to know him and his demise illustrated starkly to us the fact that coming home didn't necessarily mean you were "home free."

Smith was a short man, fairly stocky, but his size might have been a factor in his tragic end. He and his crew came back from an operational flight with one port engine out. What happened can only be surmised but it appeared that on final approach he failed to line up properly with the runway and decided to overshoot. When he opened the throttles the other engine on the port side packed in and, perhaps because of his short legs, he was unable to counteract the resulting swing to port. The kite narrowly missed the control tower and he seemed to get it levelled off but too late. It touched down on the flat roof of one of the large mobile equipment garages, skipped across a narrow drive, scraped across the roof of a second garage and plunged into the mobile equipment park where the unit's heavy vehicles and machines were kept. It burned, with him and his crew.

CHAPTER 13

Halifax VII, Autumn and Winter 1944

With the beginning of autumn we began to fly fewer tactical sorties in support of the army and returned to strategic targets. Our next operation, number 19 on 3 September, was another strike at a German night fighter drome, this one at Volkel in the Netherlands about fifteen miles from the German border. We carried nine 1000-pounders and four 500s and hit the field in daylight with only scattered cloud. The Jerries put up quite a bit of flak but no fighters. Later recce photos showed scores of hits on the runways, hangars, tarmac and barracks. On our return, Linton was again weathered in and we were diverted to a USAAF base in East Anglia.

The usual drill with the Halifax on shutting down was to open the bomb doors and lower the flaps to take the pressure off the Messier hydraulic accumulators. These cylinders stored pressure so in the event of damage there would be enough pressure to operate the flaps and bomb doors once. A similar system stored pressure for the undercarriage when the wheels were up. As we taxied in we were told not to open our bomb doors as the USAAF armourers were not trained or equipped to work on our bomb systems or our bombs if we had any hung up. Johnny was sure ours had all gone as his indicators showed all the bomb stations had fired.

One memorable feature of our overnight stay with the Yanks was that we were fed hot dogs, the only ones I saw all the time I was in the UK and they were like a letter from home! The next morning we took off to return to Linton. As each aircraft got airborne, it climbed away, wheeled and "beat up" the control tower as a farewell gesture to our overnight hosts. We landed at Linton, shut down, opened our bomb doors and a 500-pounder crashed on to the dispersal paving from one of the wing bays! I shuddered to think what would have happened if it had come off when we pulled out of our beat-up of the Yanks' control tower!

We had a hang up-on one other occasion. It was a very dark night when we landed and, as usual, we were marshalled into the dispersal site by the signals of an airman with a flashlight in each hand. As we proceeded with our shutdown drill, we saw the two flashlights suddenly take off and race across the field. We were mystified as to the reason for this until we got out and found a 500-pound bomb leaning against the port tire. It had fallen from one of the wing stations when we opened the bomb doors.

About this time our commanders realized that with the intensity of our flying since the invasion, the squadron was in danger of having all of its experienced crews tour-expired at the same time. Our crew was laid off and didn't fly for nearly three weeks while more junior crews "got some time in," as the Raf saying went. We were also given leave during which Johnny and I had a uniquely pleasant experience. We were staying at the Dorchester Hotel in London and one evening he and I were in the crowded cocktail lounge when a rather elderly couple entered, accompanied by an enormous Great Dane. They looked unsuccessfully for seats and, as we were only two at a table, we invited them to join us. The man introduced himself and the lady to us as Captain DuBois-Phillips and his wife and he gave me his card. She was terribly scarred about the face and he explained her injuries were the result of a bomb during the blitz.

Noting our Canada shoulder badges, he told us he had once been in Canada and his story went like this. He and another young man were "working on the flags in Liverpool," as he put it, meaning on the stock exchange, when they decided to go to Canada to make their fortunes. They ended up in the Yukon during the gold rush. The captain said he could stand only one cold Yukon winter and returned to England, but his friend stayed.

"You might have heard of him," he said. "His name was Robert Service."

He then launched into a rendition of *The Shooting of Dan McGrew* and entertained us for a good part of the evening by quoting Service's poetry to us. He told us he had published a book entitled *Wanderlust* but I have never found a copy of it.

Our next two ops, in daylight on the 25th and 26th of September, were again army co-op efforts, both in the vicinity of Calais and aimed at German troop concentrations. We carried our standard load of nine 1000-pounders and four 500s on both. On the first we bombed through breaks in quite heavy cloud and on the second the aiming point and markers again were partially obscured by cloud.

On the latter trip we were on the bomb run while still over England, the Straits of Dover being only about twenty miles wide at that point. We were barely over the Straits when the Master Bomber instructed us to lose altitude so we could see the target markers. I closed the throttles and stuffed the nose down to lose height as quickly as possible, while at the same time Johnny was giving me the "Left, left" and "Right, right" guidance. It was fortunate the Mk XIV bomb sight could compensate for several degrees of dive and changes in airspeed and altitude as Johnny called "Bombs gone!" while we were still in quite a steep dive. We later claimed to be the only crew to use the Halifax as a dive bomber.

A synthetic oil plant in the Ruhr at Sterkrade was our target on a daylight raid on 27 September. We carried sixteen 500-pounders on this op but as we approached the Master Bomber diverted us to Duisburg, our secondary target. Our plane seemed to be in the lead on this one and just as Johnny gave the "Bombs gone," the Master Bomber called the others back to the primary. This left us alone as we flew straight and level to get our photographs, the camera turning on at a specific interval after the bomb aimer pressed the bomb release button.

That interval seemed to go on for an eternity as we began to get radar-predicted flak. As soon as the camera had done its thing I did a 180 and then there was a cluster of bursts below and behind us, as Ralph in the rear turret informed me. I was unaware of these but had seen some a fair way off to starboard so I told Ralph, "They're not shooting at us." His reply was, "Maybe they're not shooting at you but they are sure as hell shooting at me!"

I began our textbook evasive manoeuvres based on the time it took the German gunners to reload, fire and for the shells to reach our altitude. This meant counting about fifteen seconds after a cluster of flak bursts, then turning 15 or 20 degrees and changing altitude up or down a few hundred feet. It worked like a charm and several times we saw clusters of exploding 88 mm shells about where we would have been had we not taken evasive action. In only a few minutes we were out of range of Duisburg's batteries without a scratch on the kite.

This raid exemplified the very high standard of maintenance in 6 Group. The fitters and riggers were the star performers on this one as 285 aircraft were ordered out and every one took off. When one thinks of the myriad of things that could have gone wrong with any one of the aircraft such a performance seems almost miraculous. A single example will suffice—our 285 kites required 31,920 spark plugs and their powering magnetos to function perfectly.

The Group took part in several raids in the Calais area in support of the army toward the end of September, nearly all of which were hampered by bad weather in the target areas. We were on one of these on Cap Gris Nez on 28 September and although some aircraft were instructed to abort, Johnny managed to see the target well enough for us to bomb. He unloaded nine 1000-pounders and four 500s on one of the six German batteries which were our aiming points. Calais fell to Canadian troops two days later.

The synthetic oil plant at Sterkrade seemed to be our *bête noire*. We went there again on 30 September in daylight carrying sixteen 500-pound bombs once more, only to find it cloud-covered as before. The Master Bomber directed us on to the town and several explosions and a lot of black smoke were seen. Some aircraft were able to bomb the primary through breaks in the cloud and claimed two oil tanks were set on fire.

About this time the squadron had a single Halifax Mk VI delivered to it and on 1 October I was permitted to take it up. The only way in which it differed from the Mk VII was it had Bristol Hercules 100 engines, with direct fuel injection instead of carburettors. This was intended to improve the Halifax's altitude performance. The OC asked me to see what altitude we could make. We were lightly loaded and Don timed us at twenty-one minutes from wheels up to 20,000 feet, at which point the oil cooler on the starboard inner blew out and we returned. I don't know if it ever was flown on ops.

Our next op, to Dortmund on the night of 6 October, was unusual in that it employed entirely different tactics than had been used by Bomber Command in the past. As stated by R.V. Jones in his book *Most Secret War*, by this time we had almost defeated the German radar system and, by restricting all forms of our use of electronic transmissions, had seriously hampered the German night fighters' ability to find us. In the Dortmund raid Bomber Command sent out 949 bombers (293 from 6 Group) and lost only 13 (2 from 6 Group), a phenomenally low figure for an attack on a major industrial target in the Ruhr.

The tactics we employed were to fly low across France on a heading which would indicate we were aiming at someplace much farther south. Shortly after crossing the German frontier we turned north and began to climb as rapidly as possible to a point east of Dortmund where we were to turn west and bomb the target headed for home. It worked out that way for us with one small exception which could have done us in and which at one point I strongly suspected would lead to our demise.

While flying north but still short of our planned turning point Johnny came on the intercom to say he could see the target and we should turn west. There was a very brief discussion between him, Don and me, but he was positive so I turned west to begin our run up to the target. I, too, could see a glow on the clouds ahead and assumed it was the reflection of fires in the target area. After two or three minutes it became evident we were not getting any closer and suddenly the answer came to us. We were running up on the glowing clouds covering the setting moon!

Don, on top of everything as usual, gave me a course to take us to the point from which we were supposed to start our bomb run and we arrived there many minutes late, so late in fact that we were far behind the last of the other kites in the bomber stream. Even the Master Bomber had packed up for the night.

Ahead of us a host of searchlights was sweeping the sky. Strangely, they seemed to be arranged along two lines, one on either side of our intended track. I didn't see how we could possibly avoid being trapped by them and revealed to any number of night fighters and flak guns. As we were almost abreast of the first two groups, one on either side of us, they suddenly went out. So did the next, and the next, and the next. Johnny picked an aiming point among the many fires burning below, released our load of thirteen 500-pounders, and we went home without even a stray flak gun taking a crack at us!

I have wondered about this ever since, and the only answer I can come up with is that we were so far behind the others Jerry thought the raid was over and that we were one of their night fighters. If so, they must have got quite a shock when that stick of 500-pounders marched across the target area. Johnny also saw several large explosions as we flew over. Later assessment of the bomb damage showed that all main railroad lines through the town were badly damaged as well as sidings, the steelworks and many factories.

On 14 October we were to go to Duisburg but didn't make it due to circumstances that still trouble me when I think of them. We were scheduled to take off in the late afternoon and when we arrived at the kite it became obvious that Wally and Hap had spent a bit too much time in the bar of the Sergeants' Mess. I had two options open to me— go, or abort without even starting up which would have meant certain courtmartial for Wally and Hap and the break-up of what I believed to be a damned good crew. I elected to go, believing the routine nature of our flying drills and the thoroughness of our training would make Wally's responses automatic. I was wrong and it almost killed us, but I think I would still make the same decision.

My confidence was restored to some extent when we started up. Wally went through the engine starting drill faultlessly. On a routine take-off, I would open the throttles differentially as needed to steer the aircraft until I had rudder control, at which time I'd say to Wally, "Throttles open and locked." He would then ram the throttles wide open and secure them with the locking lever so they couldn't slip back. This time, when I gave the command, he selected wheels up! This would have been the next routine command to him but his befuddled mind got them mixed up. As we were by this time going too fast and were too heavily loaded to stop before running out of runway, I pushed the throttles open the rest of the way and held them until Wally finally locked them.

Luckily, the Halifax undercarriage had a built-in safety mechanism that wouldn't permit the wheels to come up as long as the weight of the aircraft was on them. But, as we gained speed and the wings began to produce lift, every time we went over a small unevenness in the runway, the undercart attempted to crank itself up a little more. I had to counteract this by holding the nose well down and the tail high until we had flying speed. Such an attitude might have attracted attention anywhere else but we routinely performed what we called a "408 take-off," keeping the nose down and using all the available length of the runway until our airspeed was far above that needed for safe flight.

The wheels were perhaps one third of the way up into the nacelles when we got airborne with the prop tips barely clearing the ground! Just as the weight of the airplane came off there was a loud report out in the port wing. Apparently the Messier hydraulic pressure accumulator on the port wheel couldn't stand the added force put on it by the weight of the airplane pounding along the runway at speed and it blew. We got airborne without further difficulty and climbed away but the undercarriage would not react properly to any selection so we found ourselves with the starboard wheel down and locked and the port wheel down but swinging free. It wouldn't lock.

Nor would the flaps come up. As we would never be able to climb to our briefed altitude with the undercarriage and flaps in such a state, I had to abort the trip. We stooged around for a couple of hours until the time-on-target for the raid had passed then broke radio silence to tell the Linton tower of our plight. We were told to jettison our bombs on "safe" out over the North Sea which we did. Our thin-cased "cookie" exploded when it hit the water but the other thicker-shelled bombs didn't.

We returned to Linton and went through all the drills recommended to us by an engineering officer who had been called in by flying control but the state of the wheels remained the same. Then I tried every manoeuvre I could think of to try to snap the port wheel down into the locked position. However, I was told later that everyone enjoyed seeing a Halifax put through so many manoeuvres for which it was not designed—vertically banked steep turns, nearly vertical dives with pullouts as sharp as my strength would permit—but all to no avail. Flying control then instructed us to go to Carnaby to crash because they didn't want us cluttering up the runway when the other kites returned. On the way to Carnaby I instructed the crew to put on their parachutes and get ready to bail out. Howie asked me what I was going to do and when I said I intended to land the kite, all of the crew said they would not jump if I didn't.

I made a long, slow letdown and approach to the runway during which I told Wally to jettison the pilot's escape hatch above my head. He had a short struggle with it because it was stuck. I am sure I would never have been able to get it off in an emergency by myself. When he did let it go, it flew back and went edge on into the port fin where it was still stuck after we landed.

I put the kite onto the runway as gently as I could, with plenty of power on until the starboard tire touched the runway and I held the port wing up until it slowly lost its lift and settled down. I turned the magneto switches off and we rolled to a stop with a Carnaby fire truck cruising along in formation with us. I think we were all stunned by the smoothness of the landing. There was no crash, no grinding of metal on the runway, just silence!

We got out of the aircraft and soon found the reason for our deliverance. Apparently, when the Messier cylinder let go it had broken the bungee mechanism which knuckled the wheel's radius rods upward into the nacelle on retraction. Instead they had knuckled down and as the aircraft settled they jammed against the wheel hub thus preventing the wheel from going up any farther. The port prop tips were clearing the ground by about three inches, and there was no further damage to the aircraft.

Naturally, at the subsequent very brief inquiry I reported only that there seemed to be an explosion of some type in the port wing as we got airborne and that was the end of it. I was gratified by the Carnaby CO's report which stated, "A very good smooth landing. The 'freakish' accidental mechanical lock—though very fortunate—could not have stood a heavy landing. The pilot's skill and coolness is commended." But most important to me, my crew was all safe and still together. Wally and Hap never repeated their peccadillo. Nine days later we were flying the same airplane again.

This airplane became "ours" as we were now a senior crew on the squadron and we were always allotted the same aircraft for ops. It was designated "EQ-R": "EQ" for the squadron and "R" for its individual identification, or "Roger" in the phonetic alphabet of the time. I paid one of the ground crew to emblazon the nose on the port side with "Roger and Company – Exporters." This project was never finished. While we were on leave Roger disappeared. We were told another crew had landed it with the wheels up. It subsequently returned to the squadron but not in our time.

Each aircraft had its own dispersal site somewhere just off the perimeter taxi track around the airfield and Roger's was a considerable distance from the main cluster of the station's buildings. For operations we were always taken to and brought back from the site by truck but on days when we weren't flying we had to hitch rides or make our own way to the aircraft either by bicycle or on foot. I solved the transport problem for me by buying a beat-up BSA motorcycle but it couldn't accommodate the whole crew—just four of us at a time with me sitting on the gas tank and driving, one crew member on the seat, another on the back fender and one facing aft on the front fender. It wasn't properly licensed so I never took it off the station.

We solved the petrol problem by stealing gasoline from the supply the groundcrew had for the trolley-ac—with their knowledge and connivance. But the motorcycle came to an unfortunate end. While we were on leave the wireless operator with whom Don and I shared our room "borrowed" it, took it off the station at night and collided head-on with a brick wall, buckling the entire front wheel assembly past reasonable repair. My only real regret was that the borrower came out of it completely unscathed.

Our dispersal site was partially surrounded by land being cultivated by the Women's Land Army to grow potatoes. On days when we were flying and they were working this presented a problem. It was our custom, as with all aircrew, to line up along the edge of the paved dispersal pad and empty our bladders before getting into the airplane. I approached the young lady who was in charge of the group and suggested that when she saw us line up, she should have her companions turn to face away from us. This she did.

I got her name, Doreen, and address in York because she was very attractive—even in the rough breeches and khaki sweater of the WLA. Although her home was in York, she was a Birmingham University student taking time off from her studies to work with the WLA. We spent many enjoyable evenings together at the movies and dancing at the DeGrey Rooms, a popular dance spot in York. I became quite emotionally involved with her. We never were physically intimate except for a few kisses when I left her at her doorstep after an evening together. Once as I kissed her goodnight I winced as the rough sleeve of her coat scraped the back of my neck. She asked why and I explained that while flying my head was in almost constant motion as I searched the skies for other aircraft, friendly or enemy, and the back of my neck was scraped raw by the rough serge collar of my battledress jacket.

After considering this for a moment she asked me to turn my back on her. I did, and a few seconds later she was tucking smooth silk under the collar of my greatcoat. She had slipped off her panties and gave them to me to use as a soothing scarf. I wore them as such for the balance of our tour and they certainly helped cure the problem. It was a very generous gesture on her part as silk undies were almost impossible to come by in the UK during the war.

I began to think of taking her back to Canada with me when that happy time arrived, but a strange thing happened to make me change my mind. One day I was sitting staring at a picture of my Canadian girlfriend when the image suddenly blended with my mental picture of Doreen and I realized that, not only did they look alike but they were very much alike in every way, from size and build to facial appearance and personality. I decided then that my Canadian sweetheart was still uppermost in my affections.

My last flight in a Lanc II on 15 October was an air test of one of the last on the station to have undergone a major overhaul before being delivered to the RAF. A F/O Shields and I with one of his crew members and two of mine, Wally and Hap, did the test during which Shields and I decided to see just how fast a Lanc II would go. Wide open, lightly loaded, and straight and level we got it to just a fraction under 300 miles per hour, indicated air speed.

Essen was the target of my op number 26, on the night of 23 October. We carried a 2000-pound "cookie," six 1000-pounders and four 500s. The target area was completely cloud-covered and we bombed on sky markers placed by the Pathfinders. Intensive damage was done to the Krupp works as later photos revealed more than 200 of its buildings damaged and two of its biggest destroyed. As bonuses, thirteen other factories, two gasworks, two power stations, a tram depot and four railway stations were hit. This raid proved the effectiveness of new Pathfinder target marking techniques that made our night bombing as effective as daylight visual bombing.

On 28 October we went to Cologne in daylight carrying one 2000-pounder and twelve 500s. On the run-up to the bomb release point Hap called on the intercom to draw my attention to another Halifax less than a hundred feet directly above us, with its bomb doors open.

"Shall I give it a squirt?" he asked. I was tempted to tell him to go ahead and fire some tracer just in front of them, but decided against it. Their course seemed to be diverging from ours by a couple of degrees and as there was still a fair distance to go to the aiming point, they would be well clear of us by then. What I didn't allow for was a chicken crew who would bomb short. Suddenly their bombs plummeted down not more than a few yards off our port wing tip! It seemed as though that string of 500-pounders would never end. We must have been clearly visible to their bomb aimer. But it also made me wonder how many times the same thing had happened at night when we couldn't see other aircraft. Occasionally a kite was hit by our own bombs and I once saw a photo of a Hally that came back after three 500-pounders had gone right through it, one through a wing, one through the fuselage aft of the mid-upper turret and one through the opposite tailplane.

It was around this time we got a new Officer Commanding on 408, W/C J.F. "Jake" Easton, DFC. I shouldn't call him "new" because he was nearing the end of a tour on 408 and had gone through a couple of very "shaky do's." I have a picture of a Lanc II he brought home once with a jagged hole through the starboard wing about six feet across, resulting from an attack by a Jerry fighter.

Oberhausen was next on the night of 1 November. It was a bit scary because we encountered icing on the way to the target. But we were able to bomb through cloud gaps on ground markers, delivering one cookie, one 1000-pounder, four 500s and a large load of incendiaries. The raid damaged the Siemens-Martin steelworks, rolling mills, gas plants and a coking plant.

About this time another crew on 408, skippered by F/O H.D. Sokoloff, was reported missing after a raid on Bochum. They turned up a day or two later after having made an emergency landing on an allied fighter-bomber base on the continent. They had been damaged by fighter attacks. Sokoloff told us that the landing strip had been too short for a Hally and they had gone off the end but he had managed to steer the aircraft between two rows of what he, in the darkness, thought were Nissen huts. It wasn't until he was out of the aircraft that he discovered they were in the unit's bomb dump and he had steered between two rows of stacked bombs!

By this time all of my crew had been commissioned with one exception. Ralph, my rear gunner had put up a serious black involving a WAAF and a couple of service policemen whom he had laid out when they attempted to arrest him. He was tried by our CO, G/C Claire Annis and I was called as a witness. The Group Captain's questioning of me went something like this:

"You are nearing the end of your tour, are you not?"

"Yes Sir," I replied.

"Have you been flying pretty intensively?" This question was accompanied by a vigorous affirmative nod of his head with his eyes fixed firmly on mine.

"Yes Sir," I said, not untruthfully.

"Would you say your crew and this man have been under considerable nervous strain?" Another affirmative nod.

"Yes Sir," I declared.

"Would you say that this event could have been the result of that nervous strain and that it was out of character with his normal conduct?" Still another affirmative nod to me.

"Yes Sir," I averred.

There were one or two more similar questions with similar answers and the net result was that Ralph was let off with a severe reprimand rather than having to undergo a lengthy stretch in the digger, and this saved me the loss of my rear gunner. But it killed his chances of being commissioned. However, it is typical of the Group Captain's compassion for the aircrews under his command which earned the high esteem of all who served under him. He was the only CO I knew whose airmen would cross to his side of the street just so they could meet and salute him.

While we were flying so many concentrated ops after the invasion of France, the armourers found it difficult to keep up with the demand for bombs and the need to change bomb loads for last minute changes in targets. On one occasion when they were hard-pressed, the CO got on the station's Tannoy public address system and instructed everyone who was idle, regardless of rank, to lend a hand to the armourers.

Arriving at the bomb dump the CO was asked by a corporal what he would like to do. He tossed his gold-braided cap to the corporal, put on the corporal's wedge cap and said, "You're in charge here. You tell us what to do."

He had also the most fantastic memory for names and faces I ever have encountered. He seemed to greet almost every airman on the station by name. About eight years after the war I met him again in Ottawa and he addressed me by name although the trial of my rear gunner was the only direct encounter I had had with him.

We flew one more major tactical effort. This was to Julich in Germany on the Rur River west of the Rhine, in aid of the US Army which was driving for the Rhine. We carried one 2000-pounder and twelve containers of 94-pound incendiaries. The weather was good at the target. We bombed visually and the town was virtually flattened with the bridge over the Rur being demolished as well. The raid was so effective that a second which had been planned was called off by the Yanks as unnecessary.

On our next leave my navigator, Don, and I asked what was known as "The Lady Ryder Leave Club" to arrange a restful and quiet leave for us. We were sent to Waterston Manor in Dorset, not far from Bournemouth. This was the home of Brigadier General (Retired) the Honourable Viscount Dillon, CMG, DSO, Croix de Guerre (French), Croix de Guerre (Belgian), Gentleman at Arms of the King's Body Guard, etc. We arrived at the nearby railway station and were met by a chauffeur-driven Rolls Royce. Due to the manpower shortage, we soon learned that the chauffeur did double duty as the Viscount's butler.

On arrival at the Manor we were peeling off our greatcoats when the Viscount suddenly exclaimed, "I say! You two aren't doing badly, both with DSO and bar already!" We were sorry to have to disappoint him but we explained that the ribbons we were wearing were those of the "Spam and Chips," the Canadian Volunteer Service Medal (CVSM) and the "bars" were the silver maple leaves granted for overseas service. As the ribbon for the DSO is mostly dark red and that for the CVSM is green-red-blue-red-green, with the blue mostly covered by the silver maple leaf, it is possible that if the Viscount was red-green colour-blind, he could easily have mistaken one ribbon for the other.

We found the Viscount a most delightful and interesting host and we spent every evening in conversation with him in his library, to which he gave us free access. He regaled us with stories of his experiences in World War I supplemented by his photo albums from that period. We also enjoyed his beer which he imported from the Isle of Wight.

One night, as we three were going upstairs to bed, he pointed out to us two very large portraits which faced one another on opposite walls on the landings. One was of a man in eighteenth century church robes while the other was a semi-nude of an attractive young woman. He explained that the man was one of his ancestors and of the woman he said, "That was his girlfriend. I think the old boy was a bit stingy with the clothing allowance."

We spent a great deal of time just reading and resting with occasional jaunts around the estate with the Viscount. On these walks he always took a shotgun in case we should encounter a rabbit or partridge with which to supplement the meat ration, but he had no luck during our stay.

Lady Dillon was very stand-offish with us and we seldom saw her except at meal times. Of course, they dressed for dinner every night, he in black bow tie and smoking jacket and she in evening dress. Don and I both appreciated their hospitality immensely and I know the rest did us both good. But soon we were back in the real world of bomber operations.

On the night of 27 November, Neuss, an industrial area of Dusseldorf was operation number 30 for the crew except the gunners. On this one we took another pilot, F/O Dunwoodie, on his second dickey trip. It was a much more spectacular trip for him than mine had been for me as the flak over German cities always was much more intense. But it was also much more comfortable for him because of the comparative roominess of the Halifax "office" compared to that of the Lanc II.

We carried one 2000-pounder and our usual load of 4-pound incendiaries. The area was covered by thin overcast but the ground target markers were visible through the cloud. Germany's largest producer of nuts and bolts was severely battered. On the return Linton was weathered in and we were diverted to Great Ashburne, returning to Linton the next day.

Number 31 was a night raid to Duisburg. This one began badly. As I opened the throttles for take-off, the port outer engine backfired and a huge gout of flame poured out of it and over the port wing and some distance behind. I immediately closed the throttles, turned off the main north-south runway onto the intersecting east-west runway and taxied clear. We ran up the port outer and checked it again. Everything was perfectly all right.

At this point a car pulled up beside us and our foul-mouthed flight commander got in and stormed up to the cockpit wanting to know what the hell was going on and accusing me of delaying everyone's take-off by blocking the runway—which was untrue because other aircraft continued to take off behind us. I told him what had happened but at the same time I taxied down the runway, onto the taxi track, and back to the downwind end of the live runway. All the while he continued his verbal abuse but when I got a green light from the control van and turned onto the brightly lit live runway it suddenly dawned on him where we were.

"Where the hell are you going?" he asked.

"We're going to Germany. I don't know where you are going," I replied, and began to open the throttles on the brakes. He probably set a world record for getting out of an airplane in a hurry. I only hope he had to walk back to get the car he had left on the east-west runway but knowing him he probably joed some erk to do it.

We took off with our load of sixteen 500-pounders and joined the stream. It was a dark night and the target was obscured by cloud but we bombed on sky markers put down by the pathfinders, doing considerable damage to iron and steel works and the principal manufacturer of steel anti-torpedo nets.

On the way back, we were cruising along when suddenly, without any precautionary warning, Ralph in the rear turret shouted into the intercom, "Corkscrew port! Go!" followed by the chatter of his four .30 calibre Brownings. This was the usual warning of a fighter closing on us, an experience we had been spared up to this point. I rammed the control column forward and spun the wheel to the left, putting us into an almost vertical spiral dive to port. The normal completion of the manoeuvre was to descend four or five hundred feet and then spiral upwards in the opposite direction. My reflexive reaction had put us into such a steep dive that with cruising boost and revs still on we rapidly gained so much speed my strength was not able to pull us out. By the time I had regained complete control we had turned about 145 degrees and had an airspeed of close to 300 miles an hour.

Finally I managed to pull us out of the dive and get us back on course. Meanwhile there had been no other direction from the rear turret nor any more gunfire. Hap later maintained there had been no enemy attack and that Ralph, frustrated with having flown his entire tour without firing his guns once against an enemy fighter, had pulled a hoax. I still don't know what the truth was but if there was an enemy fighter behind us he's probably still wondering where the hell we went!

Hagen was our next target on the night of 2 December. This one was different because Ralph had been screened and we had a strange gunner aboard. For this trip I put Hap in the rear turret and the stranger in the mid-upper. He was Flight Sergeant Henry, and I never did get to know him although he flew with us once more. This time we again carried a cookie and incendiaries. There was some icing en route to the target with heavy cloud up almost to our bombing altitude so we were forced to bomb on H2S, our ground-searching radar. One of the principal objectives of this effort was a factory that manufactured batteries, in particular those used to drive the underwater motors of U-boats.

Two nights later we were off again, this time with two strange gunners, F/S Henry and F/S McGuire. I don't recall which one we had in which turret. The target this time was Karlsruhe, a transportation hub for both railways and canals. The target was cloud-covered but the ground markers were well-placed and visible through gaps in the cloud. Our load again was a cookie plus incendiaries, this time with the addition of propaganda leaflets asking the Germans if they wished to continue with the rule of characters like Himmler or have fair government under Eisenhower.

The most unusual aspect of this trip was that we streaked across the target with a hundred-mile-an-hour tailwind from the west. The dismal part of it was we had to fight it as a headwind after we turned for home. The tactics for which we were briefed had told us there would be a layer of alto-stratus cloud between 14,000 and 16,000 feet through which we were to descend and then hug the bottom of to give us protection from attacks from above and to our rear.

After clearing the target area on our way back, we began to descend but instead of getting down to 16,000 feet before encountering the cloud we went into it almost immediately. I decided later we had encountered a "cu-nim" or cumulo-nimbus cloud, a thunderhead. There was considerable turbulence and we began to pick up ice. We continued to descend but things only got worse and the icing became very heavy. Here the strange gunner in our mid-upper turret caused a problem. We learned later he had been a member of a crew which had crashed as a result of icing and he had been the only survivor.

With us, when his turret began to coat with ice he panicked, left the turret and was roving around the fuselage, apparently with the intention of bailing out. From my position I was unable to determine just what was going on but Wally solved the problem by going aft and laying out the panicking gunner by a blow with a fire extinguisher. Our mid-upper turret remained empty for the rest of the trip.

The ice continued to build up and we were unable to maintain altitude. We couldn't even maintain level flight but continued to descend at a goodly rate. At last we reached a level where the temperature was above freezing and the ice began to come off, clouting the fuselage noisily as chunks were hurled from the propellers. When we were able to maintain altitude Don came on the intercom to ask me in his placid fashion what my altimeter read. I told him and he replied in his usual laconic manner, "So does mine. There are hills around here higher than that." Our track was taking us across the Vosges Mountains in northeastern France. By this time we were clear of the cloud and able to regain height.

When we crossed the English coast Wally, as was our custom, handed me a cigarette and we both enjoyed the relaxation of a smoke. This made thirty-two cigarettes he had given me under similar circumstances. We made it back to base without further difficulty, landed, taxied into dispersal, shut down and got out of the airplane. I knelt and kissed the oil-soaked. pissed-on asphalt. My tour was over. I was twenty-four days short of my twenty-first birthday. But the air force didn't wean you from flying. I never again captained an RCAF airplane.

CHAPTER 14
Homeward Bound

Our first thought on finishing our tour was to celebrate the event. The five of us who remained of the original crew took the train for London. We jammed into a first-class compartment occupied only by a lone Captain of the Royal Navy pay branch. Howie indicated he had a surprise for us but first told us a yarn about it.

He had received a parcel from Canada a short time before and on opening it found, among other things, a box of corn flakes! In disgust, he snatched the box from the parcel and flung it across the room where it landed with a very audible, heavy thud. He retrieved it, opened it and found. Here he reached into his shoulder bag and pulled out a large bottle of Seagram's VO Canadian whisky, the first we had seen since leaving Canada. He opened it, passed it around and we each took a swig from it.

At last it reached the Captain and Howie invited him to partake. He took the bottle rather hesitantly, examined it doubtfully, took a small sip, and passed it on. The next time it came to him he voiced an enthusiastic, "Don't mind if I do," and took a hearty gulp! Needless to say, that bottle didn't last long.

We decided to have our celebratory dinner at Verrey's restaurant on Regent Street with which I had become familiar on 48-hour passes from Church Lawford. The dinner was a resounding success with all sorts of unrationed goodies such as wild pheasant—for a price, of course. We concluded the repast with a bottle of 1872 Madeira at a cost of something like £5. It arrived in the reverent hands of the sommelier who attempted to uncork it but the cork was so aged it crumbled and he had to decant the wine. It was so delightful we ordered another bottle but he informed us, regretfully, that we had drunk the last he had and, in all probability, the last of that vintage in Britain.

On return to Linton, Don and I were informed we would have to give up our comfortable married quarters to members of an active crew and move to a house in the village of Linton, a fair distance away. We moved but discovered the new quarters were the epitome of discomfort—cold, draughty and as it turned out, completely unheatable by the single tiny fireplace in our room.

We spent our first and only night there huddled in flying suits in front of the miserable little fireplace—after stuffing an entire box of priceless Kleenex into the cracks around the window. The next morning we moved back into quarters in the main mess building. These we were not allotted to us but as there were always some crews on leave we were able to occupy one room or another for nine-day stretches.

Shortly after our return from leave all of my remaining crew members were posted away. My gunners had been posted already to the Repatriation Depot and now Howie, Johnny and Wally followed. A few days later Don was posted to an RAF station, probably to become a navigation instructor, and I was left alone.

About this time a general mess meeting was called, the only one I recall in all my time at Linton. At the time Patton was driving for the Rhine, the British Army was approaching northern Germany, the Canadians had cleared Belgium and most of Holland and we all thought the war would be over in a matter of days. The purpose of the meeting was to prepare the mess for its return to the RAF when we vacated it.

Financially, the mess was in very good condition and in a matter of minutes we voted thousands of dollars for things such as redecorating, new carpets and so on. Our action was a bit premature. A few days later the Germans attacked through the Ardennes and the Battle of the Bulge was on. The war continued for another six months.

Christmas Eve in the mess was very quiet. Both squadrons had gone out on an op the night before and Linton was weathered in when they returned so they were diverted to another base.

Only our ground staff officers, the commissioned members of a few spare crews and screened types such as I remained. However, there was an all-ranks dance on the station so a few of us went to have a look. We danced once or twice and then three of us were invited to accompany three RCAF WDs to their quarters. They were living in permanent brick barracks that were divided into rooms, in peacetime senior NCO's accommodation.

One of my companions produced a bottle of scotch. As a matter of fact, I think it was that bottle which had precipitated the invitation, scotch being a very rare commodity. We had just nicely settled in when there was a gentle tap on the door and a voice whispered, "The Queen Bee is doing her rounds!" The "Queen Bee" was the appellation given to the senior WD officer.

My buddies and I bailed out quickly through one of the big casement windows. Fortunately for us our companions were quartered on the ground floor and we had not bothered with greatcoats or other impedimenta. It was probably the shortest party on record and the only time I used the bail-out drill. We probably set a time record for a crew of three as well.

Returning to our mess we found one type asleep in an easy chair. Our attempts to waken him disclosed that he wasn't just asleep but had passed out from overimbibing. We decided he should be taught the hazards of overindulgence in strong spirits and gathering all of the anteroom furniture, piled it in a giant pyramid almost to the two-storey-high ceiling of the room. It took some effort but we managed to carry him in his chair to the top of the pile where we left him while we went to our own beds. I would have liked to have seen his reaction when he finally came to. There were no reports of casualties the next day so I can only surmise he somehow made it safely down to floor level.

On New Years Eve a ball was held in the Officers' Mess to which I invited Doreen. She and several other invited ladies were transported to and from the station by an RCAF bus. The affair was very decorous and Doreen and I enjoyed dancing together. All were delighted by a truly sumptuous midnight repast.

Having no duties, I was able to spend considerable time in York with Doreen but on the night of 22 January I returned at about 10 p.m. to the Mess where I was greeted by the adjutant with, "Jones! Where the hell have you been? I've been looking all over for you. You had better get packed. You are leaving for Canada in the morning!"

This last bit was a slight exaggeration but at least I was posted to the Repatriation Depot in Warrington near Liverpool, the first step in the process. I left the following morning abandoning my portable phonograph, record collection, a good racing model bicycle and my beaten-up motorcycle. I had purchased the bicycle from a Committee of Adjustment, a group of officers charged with liquidating the assets of missing personnel.

My stay at the Repat Depot was short but long enough for an evening or two in Manchester and for my kit to be rifled. The only things of value to me that were taken were several books, particularly three that dealt with the misadventures of every Commonwealth flyer's "hero," the inimitable P/O Prune. His aerial antics were patterned on those of erring pilots to whom RAF Training Memoranda had awarded the Most Highly Derogatory Order of the Irremovable Finger.

Also taken were my "escape" flying boots. These last were highly prized, consisting of sheepskin-lined, ankle-high laced boots to which were attached sheepskin-lined black suede, mid-calf zippered uppers. They were known as escape boots because if one were shot down over the continent and evading capture, the tops could be removed leaving one with a pair of continental-appearing work boots. In addition, the uppers could be fitted inside a battledress jacket to provide warmth. As an aside it can be mentioned that by the time we were on ops there were so many strange uniforms captured and distributed by the Germans to workers and slave labourers that our battledress, with rank, wings and national badges removed, was unlikely to attract attention.

I embarked on the *Aquitania* and sailed on 6 February 1945 along with a host of other assorted military types and 400 British war brides. The crossing was very rough, taking eight days rather than the usual five, and in spite of the ship's forty or so feet of freeboard, we were frequently looking up at the tops of passing waves. The sight was awesome.

I have never been airsick or seasick but I came close to it once on that voyage. I was on the boat deck marvelling at the majesty of the towering waves and power of the ship when I saw an acquaintance sitting huddled in his greatcoat on a lifebelt locker. I started toward him with the intention of passing the time of day when he suddenly threw up at my feet. That was when I came close!

I remember one war bride in particular. She was an attractive young lady and showed a lot of determination during the voyage. She shared our table for meals but as soon as a plate was placed before her she would have to make a dash for the nearest washroom. We admired her spunk for at least coming to the table for every meal. One thing that was served to us throughout the voyage and which hadn't been available in England for years was fresh oranges. We gathered these up and a female companion gave them to the unlucky girl. She subsisted on oranges for the entire journey.

Again I drew duty watch, this time in company with a young English army officer. He was headed for the Far East via Canada and the US because he could speak, read and write Japanese. He was a fine travelling companion and I still have a pencil sketch he did of me.

One night while on watch we were surprised to see brilliant lights on the horizon. They were the lights of Halifax glimmering on the now relatively calm water. We stood on an open after-deck while the ship entered the harbour and watched as it tied up to a dock near the Nova Scotian Hotel. Our attempt to persuade a bosun to let us go down the gangplank just to touch Canadian soil was unsuccessful but as a result of our conversation he invited us to the Bosuns' Mess where we breakfasted on ham and eggs with freshly squeezed orange juice! We disembarked later in the morning, on Valentine's Day, 1945.

We immediately were put on a train for Montreal and on arrival went through a quick documentation process and were given thirty days' leave plus travelling time. I asked to go to Vancouver because my parents were vacationing there and was issued a travel warrant and instructions to report to Western Air Command when my leave expired.

I made the journey across Canada, stopping off in Ottawa to visit a very good school friend, who was employed by the Geological Survey of Canada. Just before I had gone overseas he had given me a sterling silver cigarette case, engraved outside with my initials and inside with the words, "Good luck Chum." Through my tour of ops

I carried it in one breast pocket of my battledress, holding my "escape" photographs. These were head and shoulder photos in civilian clothes printed on paper similar to that used by the Germans for identity photos. They were intended to be used by the French underground to make false identity papers for us when we were trying to evade capture. I still have and treasure the cigarette case although its donor has long since gone to meet our Maker.

Further on in the journey west I stopped off in Saskatoon to visit my sister, her husband and their four-year-old son. While there I encountered what became an obstacle in the path of my relationship with my girlfriend who was nearing graduation from her nurse's training. It happened like this.

One morning I went to an apartment where my Ottawa friend's wife-to-be lived. I knocked but got no reply. Thinking I would leave a note, I tried the door and it was unlocked. I opened it, and saw in a sofa-bed a beautiful girl whom I did not know. She was sound asleep and uncovered, with her night clothing in revealing disarray and her golden-brown hair spread out on the pillow.

I backed out, closed the door, and knocked again—much more loudly. A voice said, "Come in," and I did. This time she was modestly covered with bedclothes up to her chin. She looked at me a bit sleepily and said, "You're Harlo Jones, aren't you?" She recognized me from pictures shown to her by my friend's girl. It was the beginning of a happy relationship which ended—fortunately only temporarily—my association with the girl who became my wife.

My sister and I had planned to journey the rest of the way to Vancouver together and had made travel arrangements with the railway accordingly. We arrived at the station only to find that the railway, unknown to us, had changed our reservations so that my sister was booked on the first section of the train and I on the second! I can only assume this was done because I was travelling on a military warrant and the agent may have assumed it wouldn't matter to me which section I was on. I raised the roof with a reservations agent and after some argument we were re-booked together.

When we got off the train in Vancouver we were in company with several other tour-expired service types. I could see my parents standing a short way along the platform but my way was blocked by some newspaper reporters seeking comments about the war. One asked me some question I don't recall. I just brushed by him with the tossed comment that as far as I was concerned, the war in Europe was over. The next day I was quoted in the paper as having said, "The war is over!" making it sound as if I knew the war had ended. The war in Europe went on for another two months. As it later turned out, the war really was over for me even though I and all of my crew had volunteered for Tiger Force, the RCAF's planned participation in the war against Japan.

I spent the balance of my leave quietly enjoying the company of my parents, sister, my older brother and his wife and their little boy. I don't remember feeling anything other than normal but several of my friends and family told me later that my nerves were obviously pretty taut. The only indicator of bad nerves that I recall is the fact I was smoking between two and three packages of cigarettes a day.

When my leave was up, I reported to WAC HQ and was told they had nothing for me to do. They gave me the choice of either moving into officers' quarters or continuing to live in my downtown hotel. On learning that I would draw a living-out allowance, I elected for the latter and spent another two weeks or so enjoying Vancouver.

One day an air force friend and I had just come out of our hotel when we were approached by two young women who wanted to know if unescorted ladies could go into the local pubs displaying signs that read "Ladies and Escorts." We assured them they could but offered to escort them if they wished. They accepted and we began what turned into a very long and mostly pleasant day and evening in their company. They were Americans from Seattle, both quite attractive, and were on holiday in Vancouver.

We spent the afternoon showing them downtown Vancouver and Stanley Park and then took them to dinner. Later we went to the Palomar, a club with an orchestra and dance floor. En route to the Palomar we diverted to their hotel where they primped for the evening and came out with a bottle of American bourbon in one of their handbags. At that time the city's nightclubs were theoretically "dry" but the Palomar had convenient boxes attached to the underside of the tables where one could stash a bottle of liquor while ostensibly consuming only soft drinks purchased from the club. We enjoyed a few dances while partaking of the bourbon, which the young lady I was escorting did very enthusiastically.

During a pause between dances my companion asked me if I would return with her to her hotel. Believing she was concerned about finding her way in the strange city and knowing I and my fellow serviceman had every intention of seeing them safely back to their lodgings, I replied affirmatively.

In one of those sudden silences which sometimes will overtake a large gathering of people, her voice announced loudly, "Jonesy's going to sleep with me tonight!" It brought the house down. In the event, we took them back to the hotel and left my buddy's date to get her inebriated friend into the elevator and into bed.

A few days later, I was called in by WAC HQ and asked what I would like to do. When I told them I would like to keep on flying I was told the only flying job available was towing drogues for army anti-aircraft practice with a Bristol Bolingbroke. Knowing that the Bolingbroke by this time was practically an antique and also having heard that it had a decided tendency to snap roll into the ground if an engine failed on take-off, I didn't find this prospect very appealing. Also I had seen a lot of flak miss by more than the length of that tow cable. I asked what the alternative was. "A discharge," was the reply. "Fine! I'll take a discharge," I said. The next day I was on a train to Regina, the release centre nearest my home.

I was discharged from His Majesty's service on 30 April, two years to the day after receiving my wings and being commissioned. I learned later that I had been promoted to Flight Lieutenant the day I was released.

Three weeks later I was in the bush of northern Manitoba, eighty miles northeast of Flin Flon on a geological exploration party. There, one of our routine supply flights brought me a telegram informing me I had been awarded the DFC. Then came the awesome news of the atom bomb attacks on Japan and of that nation's subsequent surrender.

In an isolated bush camp with seven other men, our only contact with the outside world was a nightly fifteen-minute news broadcast on a battery-powered radio belonging to the camp cook, I sometimes felt the events of the previous three years had been only a dream.

Now, from the perspective of over fifty years, I realize I had come very close to the end of my nervous rope and it was more than a year before I got my life properly back on track, this with the willing help and support of the sweetheart of my late teens. In 1946, she became my lovely bride and the caring foundation for all of my subsequent life.

ABOUT THE AUTHOR

Harlo L. Jones was born in Dinsmore, Saskatchewan, on 29 December 1923, the fourth child of Luther and Hope Jones. At age eighteen he joined the RCAF and went to Manning Depot on 28 May 1942, two years after his second brother, Pilot Officer Dale F. Jones, RAF, had been killed in action during the British evacuation through Dunkirk. He ended the war as a Flight Lieutenant and was awarded the Distinguished Flying Cross. After the war he married his high school sweethweart, Ethel Cloake, a registered nurse. He received a Bachelor of Arts degree at the University of British Columbia, and later joined the Vancouver Sun as a reporter. In 1950 he rejoined the RCAF and served for twenty more years in Canada and Europe, retiring for medical reasons in 1970 as a Lieutenant Colonel. He then joined Saint Boniface Hospital in Winnipeg in 1971 as Materials Manager and retired voluntarily in 1974. After retirement, he and his wife travelled extensively in Continental Europe and Great Britain, East Africa, New Zealand, Australia and Fiji. They settled down in Winnipeg where, on his wife's insistence, he took up writing again and won a CBC short story contest. His first book, O Little Town was an account of youth and life in a prairie village during the Great Depression.. Harlo and Ethel have three married children and five granddaughters.